Also by R. D. Rosen

NONFICTION

Psychobabble

Me and My Friends, We No Longer Profess Any Graces:
A Premature Memoir

MYSTERY NOVELS

Dead Ball

World of Hurt

Saturday Night Dead

Fadeaway

Strike Three You're Dead

HUMOR

Bad President

Bad Baby

Bad Dog
(all co-authored with Harry Prichett and Rob Battles)

Bad Cat
(co-authored with Jim Edgar, Harry Prichett, and Rob Battles)

Not Available in Any Store

A Buffalo in the House

A Buffalo in the House

*The Extraordinary Story of
Charlie and His Family*

R. D. Rosen

RANDOM HOUSE TRADE PAPERBACKS

NEW YORK

Photo credits—chapters 2, 13: courtesy of the Nita Stewart Haley Memorial Library and History Center, Midland, Texas; chapters 3, 6, 8, 9, 10, 12, 14, 18, 19, and 23: Veryl Goodnight; chapter 5: courtesy of the Colorado Historical Society, Mazzulla Collection, no. 10035852, by R. Beinecke; chapter 7: Edwin Alderson; chapters 11, 15, 16, 22: Roger Brooks; chapter 17: R. D. Rosen; chapters 20, 21: William A. Briggs, Jr.

Grateful acknowledgment is made to Andy Wilkinson for permission to reprint four lines from "A Prairie Without Buffalo," C'aint Quit Music, Inc./BMI. Reprinted by permission of Andy Wilkinson.

LIBRARY OF CONGRESS CATALOGING-IN-PUBLICATION DATA
Rosen, Richard Dean
   A buffalo in the house: the extraordinary story of Charlie and his family / R. D. Rosen.—Random House trade paperback ed.
       p. cm.
   "Originally published in hardcover in the United States by The New Press, New York, NY, distributed by W. W. Norton & Company, Inc., in 2007"—T.p. verso.
   ISBN 978-0-8129-7888-9
   1. Brooks, Roger. 2. Goodnight, Veryl. 3. Santa Fe (N.M.)—Biography. 4. American bison—New Mexico—Santa Fe. 5. Human-animal relationships—New Mexico—Santa Fe. 6. Women sculptors—New Mexico—Santa Fe—Biography. 7. Goodnight, Charles, 1836–1929. 8. Goodnight, Mary Ann, d. 1926. 9. Ranchers—Texas—Biography. 10. American bison—Conservation—Texas—History—Nineteenth century. I. Title.
F804.S253A27 2008   978.9'5604—dc22   2007048276

Printed in the United States of America

www.atrandom.com

9 8 7 6 5 4 3 2 1

To Ellen Cathy Lewis

Man's anxiety is a function of his sheer ambiguity and of his complete powerlessness to overcome that ambiguity, to be straightforwardly an animal or an angel.

—Ernest Becker, *Denial of Death*

While we regret that the present is not like the past and despair of its ever becoming the future, its innumerable inscrutable habits lie in wait for their meaning. I want to gather them, like somebody's grandmother putting up preserves, because they will have been so beautiful.

—Diane Arbus, in a 1963 project proposal
for a John Simon Guggenheim
Memorial Foundation Fellowship

❧

Note: *Bison bison* is the scientific name for the American buffalo. The terms "bison" and "buffalo" are used interchangeably by many people, including me.

A Buffalo in the House

PROLOGUE

May 2000

He emerged into the spring morning and lay exhausted in the grass while his mother licked him ardently, freeing him from the remnants of birth. He was bright orange, almost red. For wolves and other predators, he might as well have been a neon sign in the wilderness flashing EAT, but evolution had looked after him in other ways. Within minutes of birth he would be able to stand; within an hour he would be walking. Wet and wobbly, he struggled to get up once, twice, before rising precariously to his feet on the third try. He stood there, teetering, while his mother continued cleaning him with more licks, as intently and proudly as a human mother might wield a damp washcloth on her son's first day of school. He ducked under her and found the udder, pulling on it as if he had been doing it forever, and the warm milk filled his mouth.

Nature had done him another favor by providing company. All calves came in the warm, green months of April and May. Newborns and young calves dotted his new world as far as he could see. Some of the one-month-olds, already turning brown with a dark stripe down their spines, were prancing, kicking up their heels, and jousting with each other amid the purple lupine and golden arrowleaf balsam root. But also, as far as he could see, there were grazing grown buffalo—pregnant cows, nursing mothers, and big-humped bulls—an army of protectors.

He was intrigued by all the motion and found himself stumbling among the others, drinking in the odors, sights, and sounds. The air was filled with the grunts of other mothers signaling to their wayward calves. Fascinated by his own mobility, he drifted farther away from his own mother. He approached a two-thousand-pound bull bison, sniffed him, then bunted him with his nose. The bull was majestically indifferent. In an instant his mother was by his side, reclaiming him, and he quietly curled himself around her foreleg, ready to nurse again.

That afternoon, his very first, he strayed again, sampling smells, when suddenly the great brown blur around him turned and began to move slowly in one direction. Some bulls, with their immense, serene, horned heads and their mountainous humps, pressed against him. He had no choice but to move with the powerful tide that carried him along as the air grew cluttered with grunts and guttural bellowing and filled with the dust stirred up by a thousand hooves. The commotion was terrible. He listened vainly for his mother's call. The pace quickened and his legs soon trembled with fatigue. He could not keep up. The bigger ones passed by, pushing him aside, squeezing him to the fringe of the herd, finally expelling him. He stopped, blinking, and watched as the herd moved past. Finally, he folded his legs and lay down to rest in the tall grass as the last of them, groups of mothers and their young, then an old bull or two, their coats torn and tattered, their hides scarred from ancient fights, grew small in the distance. He closed his eyes, a startling, vulnerable splash of orange in this Idaho valley.

Here he would wait for his mother.

one

Veryl Goodnight held the receiver against her ear with a shrugged shoulder while she wiped the clay off her hands with a rag. She was a well-known sculptor in bronze of animals, frontier women, and other Western subjects—and a beautiful, young-looking woman in her fifties with a soft, sibilant voice.

"It's Marlo Goble. How are you today?"

Veryl Goodnight's heart jumped. Dr. Marlo Goble was a famous orthopedic surgeon with many medical patents to his credit, and a collector of Veryl's art as well. But at the moment his key credential was that he owned the Medicine Lodge Buffalo Ranch in Idaho, just west of Yellowstone National Park. It was traditional buffalo country and the site of one of the most famous buffalo jumps, where, for thousands of years, the Plains Indians had hunted buffalo en masse by stampeding them off a bluff.

"I'm okay," Veryl said. "How are you?"

"Oh, I'm just fine. How's Roger?"

"Just fine. He's out in the barn with the horses." She glanced out the window of the studio with its Spanish tile floor and high ceiling. Beyond the barn, even though it was May in Santa Fe, there were still a few dollops of winter snow left on the foothills of the Sangre de Cristo Mountains.

"Good, good. I'm calling because I've got a two-day-old bison calf here who needs a mother. The lady postman found him yesterday wandering down by the fence on my property."

Finally, she thought. With birthing season almost over, she had just about given up hope. It had been three months since Veryl had written letters to five buffalo ranchers in the West, men who knew her and her work, asking them to let her know if and when they had a "bottle baby"—an orphaned buffalo who needed a temporary human home. Unlike genetically compromised, bred-to-be-docile cattle, mature buffalo cows were extremely self-sufficient, rarely died in childbirth, and even more rarely abandoned their young.

"What happened to the mother?" she asked, her eyes gliding over the sculpture of three wolves she was working on. Something wasn't right. Like any artist, she saw hundreds of flaws where a bystander would see only the miracle of an animal come to life in clay.

"I'll bet my cowboys were moving the herd to another pasture and they didn't notice that one of the cows had given birth.

The little guy must've gotten left behind. By the time we found him, the herd was already miles away. It's a shame, but the good news is that he got a day of nursing in. That'll stand him in good stead. You're welcome to come up and take him home for a while."

"Well, sure," Veryl said. "Absolutely. Let me find out when Roger can fly us up."

"Veryl," Marlo said, "this one's a fighter, but I can't guarantee you he's going to make it."

"I know," she replied, although she didn't know. It had never occurred to her that she might get a baby buffalo who wouldn't survive.

"First thing you need to do is go out and load up on powdered goat's milk, 'cause this little guy can sure suck the heck out of a half-gallon bottle. But, with any luck, at least now you can start that piece of yours."

"That piece" was a sculpture of a nineteenth-century rancher's wife bottle-feeding a couple of baby buffalo. Not just any rancher's wife, and not just any rancher either. Her name was Mary Ann Dyer and she had married a great-great uncle of Veryl's named Charles Goodnight. Veryl had known for years about her ancestor's illustrious career as a pioneering cattle rancher in the Texas panhandle. Goodnight was the subject of biographies, a stern but just presence in countless books on the American frontier. However, it wasn't until the past December, when a friend mailed her an article from *Texas Highways* magazine, that Veryl had learned that Charles and Mary Ann Goodnight had done something quite extraordinary: they had helped save the American buffalo from total annihilation in the 1870s.

Veryl almost immediately decided to immortalize in bronze what Charles and Mary Ann had done for all buffalo. To do that, she needed a buffalo calf, and a very, very young one at that.

She worked almost exclusively from life. For the trio of wolves she was finishing now, she had made three or four trips to the Candy Kitchen Wolf Refuge near the Zuni pueblo in southwestern New Mexico, where she had observed full-blooded wolves that had been rescued, in many cases, from humans who erroneously thought that they might make nice pets. The wolves were the most difficult subjects she'd ever undertaken. They looked so much like dogs that it was hard to capture their "wolfness." Making a wolf that looked like a dog was easy; making a wolf that looked like a wolf was not. Veryl looked over at Mickey, their Jack Russell terrier puppy, who was lying uncharacteristically still on a rug, snoozing in a patch of sunlight next to Luke, their German shepherd. Except for the occasional twitching leg, neither of them had moved a muscle in over an hour. A statue of sleeping dogs, Veryl thought—now that would be a piece of cake.

As for a buffalo calf, she knew he would be able to model for her right in her studio, as long as it was bottle-nursing, so she could symbolize the remarkable moment in American history when a few humans had nursed a species back from the brink of extinction.

Veryl walked down to the barn, where Roger was feeding his horse Kepler, who shared the barn with Matt Dillon, his other horse, and Veryl's horse Toddy. As she watched him from outside the stall, she thought, even after thirteen years of marriage: how lucky can one girl be?

Roger, retired now for several years as a commercial airline pilot, was a handsome, big-boned man, over six feet, thick as a linebacker, with a lightly freckled face red from the sun and a boyish head of graying blond hair. No one would be surprised to learn that he had once flown secret missions in Laos for the CIA, or had a first-degree black belt in karate, or still played competitive soccer. He looked like just the sort of man you'd want by your side in a war or mudslide or barroom brawl. He was exactly the kind of airline pilot you were glad to see smiling by the cockpit door as you boarded his plane.

Roger had a wry sense of humor that he indulged on rare occasions. His particular mix of openness and reserve made him entirely familiar and unknowable at the same time. When he confided in you, you were only more aware of what he *wasn't* telling you.

Roger had a gift for reading people quickly and could usually figure out within a few sentences who was capable of a real exchange of ideas and who just wanted to hear himself talk. As a result, he rarely found himself in a conversation he didn't want to be in, which saved him a lot of words. He knew how to turn aside insipid salesmen and ranting strangers with a smile. Roger hadn't married until his forties, back in the late 1980s. He was waiting for the right woman to come along. She turned out to be Veryl Goodnight, then in her late thirties, who had obviously been waiting for the right man.

"Guess what?" she asked, beaming.

Roger turned from Kepler and sized up her excitement. "You got a baby bison?" It was just like him, one step ahead of everyone else.

"Marlo Goble just called. The calf's only a couple of days old and Marlo wants us to come up and get him."

"Then that's what we'll do," Roger said.

Helped along by an MBA earned long ago at Arizona State, Roger ran the business-and-marketing end of Goodnight Fine Arts, managing everything from balancing the books and negotiating the contracts with foundries and collectors to handling mailings about Veryl's upcoming shows. He was as comfortable with the industrialists who bought sculptures as the crane operators who lowered them into place.

A couple of days after Goble's call, and all because of what had happened 125 years before in the Texas panhandle, Veryl Goodnight, Roger, and Mickey the Jack Russell terrier climbed into the turquoise-copper-and-white Cessna Conquest twin-engine turbo-prop that Roger co-owned and flew two hours north-by-northwest, biting off the northeast corner of Utah and the southwest corner of Wyoming before landing in Idaho Falls. Marlo Goble picked them up and drove them for hours up the long valley before turning onto the dirt road leading to his Medicine Lodge Buffalo Ranch. When they got out of the car, Doris Brienholt, a petite blonde who managed the ranch with her husband Stuart, was already coming toward them with her border collie. Behind them, bouncing along like just another member of the family, was an animal not much bigger than a golden retriever, and with almost the same coloring—a rusty red body and a honey-colored face. If it weren't for his broad black nose, he could have been mistaken for the long-legged family dog.

Mickey the Jack Russell, appointing himself chairman of the greeting committee, dashed up to the calf, got on his hind legs, and kissed him on the muzzle. Veryl came up behind Mickey, knelt, and took the calf's soft face in her hands. "Hi, sweetie," she said, surprised by a lick in the face. It was difficult to believe that the animal had been in his mother's womb less than a week before, and that, if he survived, he would someday become a shaggy two-thousand-pound example of one of the greatest, most haunted, and certainly most hunted species ever.

They stayed three days. Marlo, Roger, and Veryl rode out on horseback to look at Marlo's herd. Somewhere in that woolly mass of bison was a mother perhaps still wondering what had happened to her newborn. Back at the house, Doris taught Roger and Veryl how to mix the formula. In the wild, orphaned calves attach themselves to anything large and moving—as Meriwether Lewis had found out two hundred years before on his and William Clark's expedition, when a young bison attached himself to him for an entire afternoon. It was easy to see by the way the week-old calf nursed contentedly at Doris's side that he had imprinted on her. The trick now was to transfer the imprinting onto Veryl and Roger, a process helped immensely each time one of them showed the calf a half-gallon bottle of powdered goat's milk. As Veryl struggled to hold the bottle while the calf bunted and pulled, she saw that Marlo hadn't been joking about the week-old calf's appetite.

When it was time for Roger and Veryl to leave with the buffalo, Doris was so sad to see him go that she refused to make the drive back to the airport. On the airstrip, the calf polished off a bottle before Roger and Marlo herded him into a dog crate and loaded him into the cabin of the eight-passenger Conquest. Roger slid two of the chairs back on their tracks to make room. As Roger taxied for takeoff, Veryl sat next to the crate and reached through the bars to give the calf a pacifier, for which he thanked her with a soft grunt. By the time they reached the end of the runway, the calf was already asleep. Roger banked over Idaho Falls, headed south, and climbed to 27,000 feet, no doubt the altitude record for a week-old buffalo. Other than that, the flight was uneventful.

They decided to name him Charlie.

two

Charlie's namesake, Charles Goodnight, saw his first buffalo as a nine-year-old boy in the 1840s along the banks of the Trinity River, today the site of downtown Dallas. Like most people, he had been fascinated by their strength and staggering numbers. By the 1870s, Goodnight had been a Texas Ranger, legendary trail driver, cattle rancher and breeder, and inventor of the chuck wagon—and was well on his way to being widely acknowledged as "Father of the Texas Panhandle." Cattleman though he was, he was troubled by how rapidly the buffalo were disappearing; Goodnight realized that a world that had existed for thousands of years—a world that had belonged to the Indian and the buffalo—was coming to an end.

Once there had been 30 million buffalo in the United States, maybe 40. Some estimates (now considered by many to be grossly inflated) put the number as high as 80. Until 1860, even at the lowest number, there were more buffalo in America than people. At the beginning of the nineteenth century, Meriwether Lewis and William Clark had found it impossible "to calculate the moving multitude which darkened the whole plains." Another observer was more poetic: "The world looked like one robe." The country was teeming with buffalo, herds of them hundreds of thousands strong, a vast shaggy carpet of buffalo miles long and miles wide. On first seeing them, men were apt to rub their eyes and question their sanity. There were places where the buffalo weren't just on the land; they seemed to *be* the land. If you couldn't see them, you could hear them coming, well in advance, an apocalypse on hooves. Sometimes it took days for them to run past a fixed point. Some claimed you could have walked ten miles across their backs without ever touching the ground. In his memoir, the prolific buffalo hunter J. Wright Mooar estimated the Southern herd in the millions. "For five days," he wrote of a hunting trip in 1873, "we had ridden through and camped in a mobile sea of living buffalo." For much of the nineteenth century, trying to calculate their number was a favorite pastime of hunters, settlers, naturalists, and soldiers.

Over the millennia, since the last Ice Age, the buffalo had come over the Bering Land Bridge from Asia, spreading east and south. Into the nineteenth century, they roamed what are now all the states in the continental United States except Connecticut, Rhode Island, New Hampshire, Vermont, and Maine.

When the British explored Virginia in 1733, they found hordes of wild buffalo, "so gentle and undisturbed" that men could almost pet them. By the 1830s, however, the buffalo that had once roamed the East Coast from New York to Georgia had been virtually eliminated by Indians, colonists, weather, and disease.

By the 1840s, the buffalo population in the West had been whittled down as well. The buffalo on the west side of the Continental Divide were already gone, victims of the heavily trafficked Oregon Trail, with its endless wagon trains full of hungry settlers. That left the tens of millions of buffalo on the short- and long-grass prairies, but their days were numbered too.

History and progress had been conspiring against the buffalo for some time. The reintroduction of the horse to America by the Spanish in the seventeenth century gave man an animal fast enough to hunt buffalo efficiently. In the late 1600s, when the Pueblo Indians chased the Spaniards back to what is now Texas, the latter left behind some one hundred thousand horses, and now the Indians were in the buffalo-hunting business in a big way. By the 1830s, the steamboat penetrated the upper Missouri River into central Montana, opening the door to the cheap shipping of heavy goods, none more popular than the buffalo robe. Improved firearms were turning the art of buffalo hunting into an assembly-line industry. Indians had a name for the side-hammer, single-shot, extremely accurate Sharps rifle, able to drop a buffalo at several hundred yards; they called it "shoots today and kills tomorrow." The completion of the transcontinental railroad dealt the buffalo a brutal triple blow, creating easy access to the dwindling herds and more cheap transportation—after 1872, primitively refrigerated too—to the growing markets for buffalo robes and tongues in Kansas City, St. Louis, and New York. Moreover, all those railroad workers had to be fed cheaply.

The buffalo had bigger problems, of course. For one thing, they weren't cattle. The buffalo were taking up valuable grazing space and foraging land. The cattlemen couldn't wait to get rid of their "buffalo problem." Some say that homesteaders would have killed off all the buffalo eventually, to protect their farms, but the budding cattle industry was far more motivated. (The animosity toward the buffalo ran so deep in the culture of the West that, 130 years later, it would rear its ugly head in the wild buffalo's only remaining refuge, Yellowstone National Park.)

Second, buffalo weren't merely animals. Dead, they were the foundation of the entire culture of the Plains Indians—their chief source of food, shelter, clothing, fuel, ceremonial products, art, and commerce. From their skins, horns, bones, and sinew the Indians made robes, tipis, tools, combs, bowstrings, and sled runners. They had more than eighty uses for the buffalo.

The white man, of course, had exactly zero use for the Indians. The logic of Western settlement and westward expansion clicked into place; to clear the frontier of Indians—or, failing that, convert them forcibly from a nomadic into a confined, agricultural society—it would be necessary first to clear the frontier of buffalo. Although the Indians were at times wasteful consumers of buffalo, it had never been in their interest to squander the source of their survival. For the white man, fueled by political as well as economic zeal and an increasing taste for beef, the buffalo were an impediment. By the 1860s, Indians were already complaining of the wanton killing. "Has the white man become a child," the Kiowa chief Satanta asked, "that he should recklessly kill and not eat? When the red men slay game, they do so that they live and not starve."

The Indians *were* starving now, and this led to increased raids on government wagon trains, adding topspin to the vicious logic. Several famous remarks have come down to us from the 1870s to remind us that this logic was not just a construct of later historians. Army Colonel Richard Dodge reportedly told his men: "Kill every buffalo you can. Every buffalo gone is an Indian gone." More reliable are the written statements from that time. Columbus Delano, President Ulysses S. Grant's influential secretary of the interior, wrote in his 1873 *Annual Report of the Department of the Interior:* "The civilization of the Indian is impossible while the buffalo remains upon the plains. . . . I would not seriously regret the total disappearance of the buffalo from our western prairies. . . ." In 1876, when Secretary Delano's wish had almost come true, Texas Congressman James Throckmorton went on record saying, "I believe it would be a great step forward in the civilization of the Indians and the preservation of peace on the border if there was not a buffalo in existence."

As Jared Diamond has documented in his book *The Third Chimpanzee,* there had never really been any question about the direction of the white settlers' policy. "The Immediate Objectives are the total destruction and devastation of their settlements," said George Washington. "This unfortunate race," added Thomas Jefferson, "have by their own unexpected desertion and ferocious barbarities justified extermination. . . ." Supreme Court Chief Justice John Marshall intoned, "Discovery [of America by Europeans] gave an exclusive right to extinguish the Indian title of occupancy, either by purchase or by conquest." Even Teddy Roosevelt, great friend of the West, would have a word or two about the Indians: ". . . this great continent could not have been kept as nothing but a game preserve for squalid savages."

Could it get any worse for the animal once so plentiful that its herds couldn't begin to be counted? The over-harvesting of beaver led to a shift in European fashion, to buffalo robes. On top of this, a major new industrial market for buffalo hides opened up. In the winter of 1871–72, one of the biggest hide dealers of the time, W. C. Lobenstine, was asked to provide five hundred buffalo hides for an English firm that wanted to experiment with turning them into high-grade leather, something that had never been done before. J. Wright Mooar, hired by Lobenstine's agents for the job, killed 557 buffalo, sending the excess to his brother and brother-in-law in New York City and suggesting that they sell the extra hides to New England tanners to see what *they* might do.

"Even before the English firm had reported its success in the treatment of the buffalo hides, and asked for a large number of them," Mooar wrote, "I was apprised of the fact that the American tanners were ready to open negotiations for all the buffalo hides I could deliver." Overnight, turning buffalo hides into quality leather perfect for machine belting became big business. The hunters materialized, drawn by the news that a single buffalo hide might now fetch $3.50, a workingman's weekly wage elsewhere. In the 1870s, an experienced buffalo hunter could drop a hundred animals on a good day, and after expenses he could make more money doing it than Ulysses S. Grant himself was paid to be president. Army officers often passed out free ammunition and horses to anybody who wanted to lend a hand. Soon the animals' carcasses were left to rot, not even worth the effort of butchering once the bison had been skinned. As the killing frenzy intensified, many were killed—by Indians, too, now—just for their tongues, a delicacy.

For the gentry, the slaughter was presented as a game that combined the mystique of the American West and the manly allure of marksmanship. The rich—women, too—paid handsomely, even came all the way from Europe, for the privilege of shooting buffalo from fancy carriages and chartered trains. Buffalo Bill Cody, who would later become wealthy reenacting "unsuccessful" Indian attacks on stagecoaches and white settlers as entertainment (using real Indians as actors, no less), served as grand marshal for a hunt with the Russian czarevitch. The well-heeled simply removed their top hats and shawls, leaned out the windows, and fired. It was a carnival shooting gallery with real ammunition and targets. In 1869, *Harper's* magazine featured an engraving of men shooting buffalo from the windows and roof of a moving train, with the writer and illustrator Theodore Davis's verbose caption: "It would seem to be hardly possible to imagine a more novel sight than a small band of buffalo loping along within a few hundred feet of a railroad train in rapid motion, while the passengers are engaged in shooting, from every available window, with rifles, carbines, and revolvers. An American scene, certainly."

What John J. Audubon and others had predicted as far back as 1843 was a reality by the winter of 1882–83. The railroad records tell the story: In 1882, the Northern Pacific Railway moved two hundred thousand hides out of Montana and the Dakotas, but the number dropped to forty thousand in 1883, and a mere three hundred in 1884. Along the way, many had called for state laws to protect the buffalo, but only the Idaho Territory passed legislation, and it was weak, prohibiting hunting for only five months each year in an area where the buffalo were relatively scarce anyway. The Dakotas, like several other states and territories, passed buffalo-protection laws in the 1880s, but the bison were already out of the barn, and dead. On the federal level, Congress finally got around to passing legislation in 1874 to limit buffalo hunting, but President Grant promptly pocket-vetoed it.

Just as white men had been stunned by their first glimpse of the numberless buffalo decades before, many were stunned again by what they had done, and refused to believe that the animal to whom this country had belonged, as to no other, whose bountiful gifts had supported an entire civilization, was practically extinct. The vast carpet had been reduced to an endless blanket of bleached bones destined for fertilizer, carbon black, and fine bone china for the carriage trade. Teddy Roosevelt told of a rancher who, crisscrossing the length of northern Montana, was never out of sight of a dead buffalo, or in sight of a live one.

The photographs of massacred bison and stacked hides gave way to photos of piles of buffalo bones in factory grounds. In one famous image from the 1880s, a man at the Michigan Carbon Works in Detroit stands atop a mountain of buffalo skulls forty feet high. At the bottom of the mountain, another man poses for the camera, a foot perched on a buffalo skull plucked from the pile. Though not the hunters, the men nonetheless look triumphant, proud to play even a small role in the buffaloes' demise. It's as if they are the beaming curators of an exhibit of man's victory over nature. *Buffalo? What buffalo? We didn't see any buffalo.* America was a land of plenty, including plenty of bones that used to be buffalo. No one was going to let a small thing like 30, 40, 50 million buffalo get in the way of a destiny as manifest as America's.

In one form or another, bison had been on the earth for almost a million years. Between ten thousand and thirteen thousand years ago, at the end of the Pleistocene Era and the last Ice Age, almost all of the several giant North American animals—fifty-foot-long alligators, ten-foot-high carnivorous birds, and 1,500-pound guinea pigs—became extinct, as a result of hunters, climate changes, and possibly other natural catastrophes. Huge horses, camels, woolly mammoths, mastodons, saber-toothed cats, and giant short-faced bears were, after surviving almost two dozen other Ice Ages, suddenly gone forever.

Only one of the bigger beasts survived: the buffalo. What climate changes, evolution, and four-legged predators couldn't accomplish for hundreds of thousands of years, humans nearly did over the course of a few decades.

IN OCTOBER 1876, when the Great Slaughter was well along, forty-year-old Charles Goodnight laid eyes for the first time on

the Palo Duro Canyon in the Texas Panhandle. He had seen no
buffalo on the tableland, so he was surprised to find ten or
twelve thousand of them grazing on the canyon floor. But he
was less interested in buffalo than in cattle; he was about to establish the first ranch on the Texas Panhandle, the JA, in part-
nership with an Irish financier named John Adair, and he
realized he was looking at the perfect place to do it.

Where once it was covered with enough grass for both cattle and buffalo, today the ten-mile-by-hundred mile Palo Duro
is overgrown with cedar, scrub oak, mesquite, and yucca. The
JA is still in operation, the oldest continuously owned ranch in
the Panhandle. Its owner, Ninia Ritchie, who is descended from
John Adair, has a state-of-the-art kitchen in the greatly expanded main house, stocked with food and delicacies from all
over the world, and if she needs shallots or Bibb lettuce, all she
has to do is drive along the canyon's rim to towns like Claude
and Clarendon. However, when Charles Goodnight brought
his wife Mary Ann—he called her Molly—down from Colorado to be with him, the place might as well have been Mars for
all the amenities it provided.

Charles, whose great-grandfather had come from Germany
and settled in Virginia in the 1750s, always thought he had
married above him. Mary Ann Dyer was a schoolteacher whose
family included a governor of Tennessee. She was a strong, independent woman who had raised her two brothers after their
parents' deaths. Mary Ann didn't frighten easily. But at the end
of the trip to the Palo Duro, when the traveling party camped
one night with its 1,600 head of cattle on a mesa overlooking
the canyon, she heard a sound that scared the wits out of her, a

terrible rumbling coming closer, clearly soon to engulf them. Charles finally convinced her it was only a stampede of bellowing buffalo that, despite the roar, was a mile or two away in the canyon. "Mrs. Goodnight, not being accustomed to such scenes, became greatly alarmed, saying they would run over the wagon," Goodnight would say many years later. Not only could he see that she wasn't fully convinced, but an actual thunderstorm promptly began, so he built a blazing fire, "assuring her that buffaloes would be easier turned by a light than a cavalry charge." As she cowered on top of the mesa, Mary Ann would have been surprised to know how big a role buffalo were to play in her life, and she in theirs.

The next day, Goodnight drove the cattle down the narrow entrance to the canyon. "As the canyon widened," he remembered, "the buffalo increased till finally by the time we arrived at the upper end of the wider valley . . . we supposed we had ahead of us ten thousand buffaloes. Such a sight was probably never seen before and certainly will never be seen again, the red dust arising in clouds, while the tramp of the buffaloes made a great noise. The tremendous echo of the canyon, the uprooting and crashing of the scrub cedars made one of the grandest and most interesting sights that I have ever seen. If they did not come off the mountain sides that were near us we simply sent a sharp-shooter ball amongst them. A nearby shot caused an instant stampede, making kindling wood of the small cedars as they came."

In a two-room log cabin, still standing today as the oldest part of the sprawling JA ranch house, Mary Ann Goodnight tried to make a home, the first in the Texas Panhandle. She lived in a world of howling winds and cowboys who didn't say much. She patched their clothes, sewed on their buttons, treated their illnesses and injuries, and tried to engage them in small talk. Her isolation was so great that a sack of three chickens utterly transformed her social life during that second winter. When a cowboy brought them by one day, she knew better than to cook her new feathered company. "No one can ever know how much pleasure and company they were to me," she would reminisce. "They were something I could talk to, they would run to me when I called them, and follow me everywhere I went. They knew me and tried to talk to me in their language."

She eventually imported what she could from civilization, including a New York artist she commissioned to travel down to Texas to paint local landscapes that she could hang on her walls. Her husband, however, was aware of what he had gotten her into, and many years later he gave her a clock inscribed:

IN HONOR OF

MRS. MARY DYER GOODNIGHT

PIONEER OF THE TEXAS PANHANDLE

For many months, in 1876–1877, she saw few men and no women, her nearest neighbor being seventy-five miles distant, and the nearest settlement two hundred miles. She met isolation and hardships with a cheerful heart, and danger with undaunted courage. With unfailing optimism, she took life's varied gifts, and made her home a house of joy.

Mary Ann survived the first couple of winters and even came to love the rugged, demanding life of a rancher's wife. She would later view these years as among the most exciting she had ever known—made even more suspenseful by the occasional unscheduled visit from Comanches or Kiowas. Her trepidation about hostile Indians was eased greatly by her husband, a man of great integrity and tough compassion who treated Indians fairly, was treated fairly in return, and made several lifelong friends among them. Mary Ann's other fears—of buffalo stampedes, rattlesnakes, the merciless winter winds, and the great isolation—also gradually abated.

There was one thing, however, that she never got used to: the endless killing of the buffalo. Day after day, she could hear the reports of the new long-range breech-loading rifles— the "Big Fifty" .50-caliber Sharps and the Remington—that had been added to the list of the buffaloes' woes. The rifles were followed by the buffalo skinners, whose teams of horses would pull the buffalo hides clean off them, then dry them on stakes, flesh side up. As Mary Ann did her chores, preparing simple meals and conversing with her chickens, she was haunted by the guns in the distance.

Mary Ann, who was childless, asked her husband if he would rope out a couple of orphaned buffalo calves for her before it was too late. She would try her hand at raising them herself, safe from the sharpshooters and the safaris. Charles was a practical man; at first, he didn't think much of his wife's idea. After all, he was a cattleman. On the other hand, he had great respect for the buffalo, which he believed to be smarter than the horse, the antelope, and the cow (except, perhaps, when it came to a propensity to go through, rather than around, fences and bodies of water). Buffalo, he had observed, never used deception to protect their young, but confronted their enemies and fought without regard for their own safety. They could go twice as long without water as a cow could, and could smell a water source from miles away if they were downwind of it. Not only did they eat about a third less grass than cows, but, thanks to two more incisors, they were better at finding and eating it. In winter, buffalo used their heads, massive neck muscles, and beards to whisk away snow to reach dead grass that cows couldn't find. Neither wind, water, nor cold could penetrate a buffalo's dense coat. Its hair held so much heat that on a sunny winter's day you could put your fingers down into its coat and barely keep it there, it was so hot. Unlike cattle, which during severe storms tended to drift to low spots and get trapped or buried, buffalo survived by facing *into* the storm. Sometimes they'd even head slowly *into* a storm, shortening their time in it. In warmer weather, the animal was a highly efficient roughage feeder—a veritable mowing machine—as well as an ecological miracle: Unlike cattle, who wore grooves in the soil, killing the grasses, buffalo grazed in tight, wandering herds, eating the grass down to the soil, then moving on, giving grassland as much as two years' rest before they came around again. In the spring, they rolled around, shedding grass seeds caught in their coats since the previous fall. They *replanted* the soil. They gave back, fertilizing the prairie with their nitrogen-rich urine and, eventually, their decomposing bodies. (It would be another 130 years before their ecological importance to the grasslands was appreciated by a new generation of scientists and preservationists committed to the dream of restoring the American prairies.)

Charles Goodnight, in fact, had actually tried to start a domestic herd a dozen years before. The mother of one of the calves he roped out had attacked him so savagely that he had had to kill her to save his horse—an act for which he never quite forgave himself. Eventually he gave his six buffalo calves and their foster-mother cows to a friend to raise for a 50 percent stake in the herd, but the friend lost interest, sold the herd, and never gave Goodnight his cut. The whole affair left a bad taste in his mouth. Still, he thought, waste was a sin—his cowboys used to scatter nails around the ranch just to see Goodnight pick them up—and what was happening to the buffalo offended his moral nature. Goodnight was also a loving husband. So, between one thing and another, he presented Mary Ann with two yearling buffalo, a male and a female, soon to be joined by four more.

Mary Ann bottle-nursed the six calves until they were strong. A few more came along, and some of them started having calves of their own. The years passed and Charles Goodnight's cattle ranch and prosperity and fame grew, and so did their little herd of buffalo. It grew to fifteen animals, then thirty, sixty, a hundred and twenty. By the time Charles Goodnight died in 1929, the herd numbered two hundred and fifty.

The vast majority of the North American buffalo alive today are descendants of a few wild survivors who took refuge in Yellowstone and about eighty calves that were hand-raised 120 years ago in Montana, Manitoba, and the town of Goodnight, Texas.

three

The other animals' reactions to Charlie were mixed. From the beginning, Luke and Mickey considered him to be just another dog, an assumption destined to cause them a certain amount of confusion a few months down the road. The four Goodnight-Brooks cats displayed a sublime indifference. The horses seemed equally unfazed, but then they didn't get to see much of Charlie because, although he slept in the barn in a stall between Matt Dillon and Kepler, for the first few weeks he spent almost all of his time in and around the house.

As a result, Charlie began developing a rather unusual skill set for a bison calf. Instead of learning his way around the grazing land at the Medicine Lodge Buffalo Ranch, charging other bull calves in harmless imitation of the sometimes fatal showdowns between rutting adult bulls, enjoying dirt baths, and taking instruction in what to do when a wolf patrolled the herd's perimeter, Charlie was getting to know the roughly landscaped yard of an adobe-style house outside of Santa Fe, New Mexico, learning the best place to nap in Veryl Goodnight's studio, and occasionally charging a Jack Russell terrier who thought he was much bigger than he actually was.

Most of all, he nursed. The zeal with which he pursued a strict schedule of four feedings a day removed any doubt about his general health. For the first three weeks, Charlie was able to combine his favorite activity with the purpose for which Veryl and Roger had obtained him: He spent part of every day modeling for Veryl's clay study of Mary Ann Goodnight bottle-feeding her first two buffalo calves back in 1878. Veryl was going to call it "Back from the Brink." Veryl's longtime model Jessica Lacasse would arrive just before feeding time and slip into a replica of a late-nineteenth-century dress and apron that a local seamstress had made from period photos. Veryl had Jessica use a glass milk bottle from the nineteenth century that she'd found at an antique store; since Charles Goodnight didn't knowingly allow liquor on his ranch, Veryl figured that Mary

Ann wouldn't have used a liquor bottle to nurse her calves. Charlie would curl his body around Jessica, reach for the nipple, and nurse contentedly while Veryl worked on her clay study.

By the time he was a month old, however, Charlie was already a bit of a challenge to feed. Jessica could no longer handle him, and even Roger and Veryl were beginning to have trouble. He'd bunt and butt and work the rubber nipple so hard that if they held the half-gallon bottle of goat's milk too tightly he'd rip the nipple off. If they didn't hold it tightly enough, the bottle itself had a tendency to go flying across the room. And if they held it with just the right degree of tension, they'd be laughing so hard for the whole two minutes it took Charlie to polish off the bottle that, on that account alone, it wasn't easy to finish the job. When the bottle was empty, Charlie would look at them impatiently and start pounding his hooves in a ridiculous sort of tap dance, and they would crack up again.

When Charlie was no longer modeling on a regular basis, Roger discovered that the calf wanted to follow him everywhere—around the house, to the top of the driveway to get the mail, into the yard. While Roger read the paper on a lawn chair Charlie would sniff him, or he'd curl up with him for an afternoon siesta. When he couldn't be *with* Roger, he'd be as close as he could. When Charlie was outside and Roger was working in his ground-floor office, where he ran Veryl's business, kept in touch with old friends in the military-intelligence community, and now spent some of his time studying the history of the buffalo, Charlie would walk over to the flower bed right under the office window, crush a few dozen flowers, and take a nap. The property was already fenced, except for the end of the driveway, where Roger now installed a gate they could open electronically from the house. But Charlie had no interest in going anywhere that Roger wasn't.

Whenever Charlie sensed Roger in the vicinity, he'd let out a grunt—what bison biologists refer to as a "contact call"—a kind of "Here I am." But he communicated primarily by "kisses," which involved a rather large amount of licking and saliva. Although Roger was the principal object of Charlie's amorous attention, Charlie used every opportunity to flirt with visitors to the house, of whom there were of course more than usual, now that word had leaked out that Roger and Veryl had given new meaning to the term "house pet." Many guests who weren't paying sufficient attention to their surroundings were surprised by the appearance of an enormous, scratchy buffalo tongue that, with a couple of licks, could leave one's forearm red for a day or two. Veryl would apologize; she felt responsible for Charlie's poor manners. During Charlie's first couple of weeks, Veryl would enter the barn with a handful of carrots in the morning and greet him and the horses by name. Since Charlie was too short to reach the feed door, he'd thrust his muzzle up toward Veryl's hand, and she'd ask for a kiss before giving him his carrot. He'd been in a Pavlovian salivation frenzy ever since.

Roger was surprised but pleased to find himself so suddenly at the center of Charlie's life. The dogs really belonged to Veryl, the horses lived their lives of quiet dignity in the barn, and the cats belonged mostly to themselves, but Charlie could not have found Roger more fascinating, and the feeling was increasingly mutual.

ONE OF THE GREAT BONDS between Roger and Veryl was their mutual love of animals. Their lives were filled with real animals, their house with paintings and sculptures of animals by Veryl and other artists. In the yard there were more bronze animals, including a statue of four mares and a stallion bursting in a gallop out of the rubble of the Berlin Wall—the model for a larger-than-life-size, seven-ton bronze piece by Veryl that is now installed at the Allied Museum in Berlin. Their wedding photo showed them on horseback. A fair percentage of Veryl's wardrobe consisted of clothes featuring horses, dogs, and cats. Her dishware had horses on them. Her notepaper said "You herd it here first" under a drawing of galloping horses. She had grown up watching *Lassie, Rin Tin Tin,* and *My Friend Flicka,* and reading Albert Payson Terhune and Walter Farley. Forty years later, her love of animals still dictated her choice of reading matter. She had been raised in a modest neighborhood just west of Denver, rural at the time, and one of her first memories was of wanting a horse, which her parents could not afford. Whenever she could, she took grass cuttings to all the neighborhood horses. In the winter, she created her own horses in the yard, learning their form with one mittenful after another of Colorado snow. When her steeds melted each spring, she could not hold back the tears.

She and Roger had met on horseback thirteen years before. Roger was decompressing from a flight, as he often did, by driving out from his home in Denver to Castle Rock, where he boarded Kepler, his bay Anglo-Trakaner, and rode him out into the hills toward Dawson Butte. He relished these rides, all the more so because airplanes were so dependable, every mechanical input by the pilot matched by a response. Their circuitry was largely infallible. By contrast, horses were almost human, prone to inexplicable deviations. Roger, who was fascinated by the complexities in any relationship, found this unpredictability a refreshing challenge. As he cantered Kepler across the crest of a hill on this particular evening, an elk herd in sight, he spotted another rider in the distance. When their trails later converged and he discovered the rider was an attractive woman astride a small white Arabian horse, he rode Kepler over.

"I've never been on a horse that big," Veryl Goodnight said to Roger Brooks when he pulled up.

"I've never been on one that small," he replied.

"That's a lot of horse."

"See for yourself—if I can ride that little Arabian of yours."

They traded their horses' names—hers was Gwalowa—and then they traded horses.

She wasn't overly impressed, riding Kepler. Veryl believed that Gwalowa, whom she'd once ridden to victory in a fifty-mile endurance race, was the reincarnation of the horse of an Indian warrior. "Is he green?" she asked Roger.

"No, he's a bay," he said, pretending to have misunderstood. For a moment she thought he might be a bit of a dolt, but she gave him the benefit of the doubt, in part because he was one of the better-looking men she had ever met.

"So what do you do?" she asked.

"Airline pilot. You?"

She said she was a sculptor, currently working on a monument.

"Isn't that depressing?" he asked after a moment.

"What?"

"Making headstones."

"Not that kind of monument. It just means a bigger-than-life-size sculpture." He couldn't be *that* dense, she thought.

"You live out here?" he asked.

"Not too far away."

"Family?"

"Seven horses, a border collie, a pygmy goat named Joe the Wrangler, and a prairie dog named Petey."

"A prairie dog?"

"Someone left him at the gate of the Denver Zoo, and I was the first person they thought to call."

"You've got that kind of reputation, huh?"

"What I've got is a license for wildlife rehabilitation."

"So what do you do with a prairie dog?"

"Oh, he hangs around the house. Sleeps with me at night."

"Come on."

"Don't knock it if you haven't tried it."

"Does he have a sister?"

This time she laughed.

He managed to get an invitation to Veryl's house on the pretext of having to meet Petey, who was not pleased to be introduced to the new competition and quickly made himself scarce. When Roger was about to leave, saying his good-byes to Veryl at the door, Petey finally reappeared, got on his hind legs, and started chattering, "Whee-poo! Whee-poo!"

"What's 'Whee-poo' mean?" Roger said. " 'Thank God the big guy's leaving!'?"

"Well, *I'm* a little sorry to see you go," Veryl said.

He took Veryl's face in his hand and kissed her lightly on the lips. "That's for Petey," he said.

Veryl pulled his face toward her with both hands and kissed him good and hard on the mouth. "And that's *from* Petey."

After a few more dates on horseback, they continued their courtship in a car. Roger, who was very curious about Veryl's art, insisted on driving her to Oklahoma City to deliver a life-size sculpture of a mare and foal called "Paint Mare and Filly." Once there, he insisted on working with the crane operator to position it properly. Before long, Roger was an expert on monument installations and Veryl was something of an expert on Roger. As things progressed between Roger and Veryl, her relationship with Petey began to deteriorate. Petey wouldn't share Veryl with Roger, expressing his displeasure in the form of incessant chattering and occasional attacks on Roger's lower body, and this resulted in Petey's exile to the basement.

ALTHOUGH THEIR LIVES revolved around domestic animals, Veryl and Roger had no illusions about wild ones. In both Colorado and New Mexico, Veryl had held wildlife-rehabilitation licenses, granted only to those with wildlife-handling experience, the right temperament, and the facilities to take in wounded or abandoned wild animals on a temporary basis. Roger was an accomplished horseman who knew his place in the animal kingdom. Both of them scoffed at people who romanticized the ownership of wild animals; it was consumerism at its most pretentious. Americans keep an estimated ten thousand tigers, many as pets—a figure thought to be twice the estimated number of wild tigers. Roger didn't approve, although he could understand the appeal. What was a Bugatti or a Picasso—or anything money can buy—compared to the beast who overcomes hundreds of thousands of years of evolution to make the leap into the world of humans? The rare beast who, indifferent to all other humans, has chosen to bless you with its affection?

Since 1998 alone, there had been no fewer than seven fatal tiger attacks on humans in the United States, two of them on small children. A cute month-old buffalo calf could be considered an accident just waiting to grow up. Because so few people have ever claimed them as "pets," no one bothered to keep statistics on acts of buffalo aggression against humans—except in Yellowstone National Park, where between 1980 and 1999 bison charged and struck seventy-nine people, with one death and many injuries. Yellowstone offered visitors bright-yellow warning flyers with a tasteless but effective drawing of an airborne child who's just been launched by the horns of a bull bison, and the reminder that "Buffalo weigh 2000 pounds and can sprint at 30 mph, three times faster than you can run." You didn't have to spend more than a few seconds near the horns of a domesticated bull bison to recognize how little effort it would take a peevish buffalo to radically change a life. A hundred years ago, an Idaho rancher named Dick Rock raised a buffalo from infancy, only to be gored to death by him. An old photo of Rock proudly astride the animal in better days was all the lesson you needed in human hubris, Large Mammal Division. In the late nineteenth century, one of the two buffalo bulls trained by A. H. Cole to pull a cart on his Nebraska ranch fatally impaled his master on a horn.

As the Department of the Interior's Wildlife Leaflet 212, *Buffalo Management,* puts it, "Regardless of the extent of handling and of apparent domestication, buffalo are *dangerous wild animals* of uncertain temperament and should never be trusted. Supposedly tame animals have attacked owners caught off guard. *Buffalo are not suitable for pets or mascots.*"

Roger and Veryl understood they weren't adopting a calf, just borrowing one. They had no desire to be the owners of an adult trophy bison. They knew it was only a matter of months before Charlie's true nature would begin to emerge and he would have to return to Marlo Goble's ranch in Idaho, his modeling career safely behind him.

four

Unlike Petey the prairie dog, Charlie seemed to have little interest in sharing Roger and Veryl's bed. As the days of summer wore on, he ingratiated himself to both human members of the family. He expanded his diet from powdered goat's milk to include the grass in the yard around the house, releasing Roger from his lawn-mowing duties. Unfortunately, Charlie also developed a taste for flowers—any flowers. He ate them with the intensity of a nervous party guest left alone with the potato chip bowl. With solid food in him, he began to indulge in the age-old bovine activity of turning partially digested wads of grass into carbohydrates and fatty acids—otherwise known as chewing his cud.

"Back from the Brink," Veryl's sculpture of Mary Ann Goodnight bottle-feeding one buffalo calf while a second looked off into the distance, was coming along nicely. Since Charlie was too big and restless to sit still in the studio, when Veryl needed to refer to him she'd head for the corral. She'd set up there and work on whatever part of Charlie he happened to be showing her. If he happened to be facing away, showing her his butt, then that is what she worked on. Once in a while, though, it was Charlie who came to visit her. One afternoon, while Veryl was in her studio working on the sculpture, she saw something move out of the corner of her eye and looked up. Charlie was standing outside the big studio window, watching her work while he chomped on fallen peaches, pits periodically dribbling out of his mouth.

Although his active modeling career was over, Charlie still spent a substantial amount of time inside the house those first few months. He had learned to negotiate the terra-cotta floors, drink out of toilets, and find his way to the kitchen to check out the fruits and vegetables in the bright blue bowl on the counter. At some point, though, he began to have trouble maneuvering in tight spaces such as Roger's office. Inevitably, one day Charlie moseyed in there, couldn't quite turn around, and, rather than back out, forced himself to complete a 180, wiping Roger's desktop clean in the process with a swish of his increasingly large head.

"Charlie," Roger said, surveying the damage, "I'd appreciate it if you showed my desk just a little more respect."

There were more problems. In early August, while Veryl was working in the studio, Charlie, who was now the size of a dusty brown Great Dane, climbed on the couch in Veryl's studio to take a nap. When he got up an hour later, he left behind a wet spot about the size of the Abiquiu Reservoir.

It was pointless to get mad at him. Clearly, if you wanted things just so, it was foolish to keep a buffalo in the house. But Roger was enjoying Charlie more and more. When Veryl first mentioned the idea of temporarily hosting a buffalo, he had gone along with it, not unlike Charles Goodnight had with Mary Ann's suggestion. Veryl needed a baby bison for her art, and what was another temporary guest in a relationship that had accommodated more than its share of species? But Charlie, he gradually realized, was becoming much more than a responsibility, or even a novelty. Roger began to look for Charlie when he wasn't around, and to bask a bit in his presence when he was. Charlie had started taking up some of the slack in Roger's life. The buffalo was beginning to provide some necessary resistance, like a good headwind, that had been missing.

Charlie was amazingly good-natured and sweet-smelling. Roger thought he smelled like fresh laundry. He smelled better than the dogs and the cats, and was better company, too. So it saddened Roger when it began to dawn on him and Veryl that Charlie was getting too large for the house. Roger was not interested in spending too much of his valuable time blotting up bison urine. And he knew what the odds were that Charlie would evolve into an acceptable houseguest.

When Roger was a boy in California, his Texas-born father, a two-packs-of-Camels-a-day car dealer, a gentleman golfer and gambler, had a habit of singing "Home on the Range" around the house. It was his entire repertoire, and the tedium of it had been such that Roger had never been able to bring himself to sing it. Yet now, suddenly, he caught himself humming it. That was bad enough, but the lyrics soon drifted unbidden into his head: "Oh, give me a home where the buffalo roam / where the deer and the antelope play / where seldom is heard a discouraging word / and the skies are not cloudy all day." Roger figured there had to be a powerful reason for so rejected a song to force its way into his head, and he knew what it was. Home for buffalo had pretty much always been on the range, not inside a nice faux-adobe house. But no one had bothered to tell Charlie that. And he was about to hear some very discouraging words.

"Charlie," Roger said one afternoon when Charlie was waiting at the front door for Roger to let him in, "we need to have a little talk."

Roger was not unaware that he now spent a portion of every day talking out loud to a bison. The fact was that, since he had stopped flying commercially, some of his most interesting conversations were with animals. It amused him that some people liked to say that animal lovers were just "compensating," as if the love of animals was some slightly unnatural act that could only be explained as a function of flaws in some other relationship.

"It's like this, Charlie," Roger said, stepping outside. "You're tipping the scales at more than four hundred pounds." They started walking together down toward the barn and the arena. "You're bumping into things. Every few days you wipe everything on my desk off onto the floor. You recently used the sofa in Veryl's studio as a potty. Let's go down to your corral."

Charlie started down the path ahead of him.

"Veryl and I have been talking and we think it might be time for you to confine your activities to the out-of-doors." They walked a little more. "It's not that we love you any less than before, but, son, you're just too damn big to be in the house."

Charlie kept walking, indifferent to Roger's views. He was almost at the gate to the corral, or arena.

"All right," Roger suddenly blurted. "You win. But mark my words. I'm going to put my foot down pretty soon and then your indoor days are going to be over."

That night, the very night of Charlie's reprieve, Roger and Veryl were entertaining a real-estate magnate named Takeharu Miyama, a major collector of her work who was visiting America with his elderly parents. The Miyamas were very excited about meeting Charlie. A buffalo for a house pet! Imagine that! What would those crazy Americans think of next?

"Come on, Charlie," Veryl said, coaxing him down the hallway. "Come say hello to our friends."

When Charlie turned the corner from the hall, he became excited at the sight of Takeharu and his elderly parents sitting on the sofa in the living room. His hooves started slipping and sliding and clattering on the Mexican tile floor. For a few seconds, he looked like a cartoon, all furiously spinning legs and no locomotion. When his legs finally got traction, they began to carry him quickly toward the sofa. He was making a charge, however unintended, at the visitors. Take and his parents scattered in every direction—exactly what people had been doing for thousands of years at the sight of a charging buffalo.

Veryl was less worried about the visitors—now safely hidden behind pieces of furniture—than that Charlie would have to jump over the couch and onto the table behind it, on which she kept a very valuable glass punch bowl. Instead, Charlie came to a noisy halt in front of the couch, walked calmly around it and then straight into the table, knocking off the punch bowl, which shattered into a thousand pieces.

Charlie looked at Veryl and Roger with his big dark eyes, as if to say, "What are you looking at? What did *I* do?"

And that was the last time Charlie was allowed in the house.

So Charlie started coming into the house without an invitation.

One summer day shortly after his banishment, he pushed his wet nose right through the screen door and strutted smartly through the foyer and up the stairs. By the time Veryl found him, he was in their bedroom, standing on top of their king-size bed, looking as if he might be posing for a mattress ad whose copy read something like: "For our mattresses, a couple of kids bouncing on the bed is nothing."

Veryl was annoyed, but not surprised. By the time a buffalo

bull is grown, he looks as if he's been made from other animals' spare parts—a camel's hump, a pit bull's aquiline profile, an elephant's rib cage, the slim rump and hind legs of a lion. The whole bearded effect is somewhat amusing, like a bodybuilder with atrophied legs or a barrel-chested brute working as a runway model. You would never guess that the whole buffalo is a lot faster and more agile than the sum of its parts. The best can outrun a quarter horse at his own race. More impressive still, they can jump six feet into the air from a standstill. Jumping *down* seems to hold the same fascination for them, but it's one of the few areas in which buffalo seem to suffer from a lack of common sense. They are known to jump off bluffs ten and fifteen feet high rather than go a little bit out of their way to get where they are going.

For a calf Charlie's age to climb stairs and hop onto a bed was pure fun, and he tried it again. Veryl heard him bust through the screen from her studio and yelled out, "Charlie's through the door!" Roger darted out of the kitchen, where he had been reading the Santa Fe *New Mexican,* reached the stairs just ahead of Charlie, dashed up to the second floor just ahead of him, and closed their bedroom door before Charlie had another chance to try out their mattress and box spring.

It was hard not to believe that Charlie was trying to invent a game. The playfulness of buffalo in the wild is well known, beginning with a male calf's tendency to pick fights with elders twenty times his own size. Adult buffalo have been observed ice-skating on frozen rivers and playing soccer with hay bales. In the 1880s, a cowboy named Charlie Norris found a group of older bison jumping off a steep bank into a creek, then paddling back to shore, where they would climb out, scamper up the bank, and jump off again.

"He thinks he's a person," Veryl said to Roger after the second broken-screen episode.

"No, honey," Roger replied. "Charlie thinks we're buffalo."

Veryl had to laugh. "Then I wonder what he'll think buffalo are."

A new lock and some reinforced screen for the front door finally put an end to Charlie's unexpected visits. To make it up to him, Roger began taking more and more walks with Charlie in the foothills of the Sangre de Cristo Mountains, among the scrub oak, cedar, juniper, sagebrush, and piñon pine. As with most things involving Charlie, a walk was no ordinary experience. Some days, Charlie seemed to be in a big hurry, nosing Roger down the path, making him hustle to stay ahead of Charlie's budding horns. Once, when Roger didn't move fast enough, Roger received what could only be called a buffalo wedgie when Charlie hooked the knob of one of his horns in the back of Roger's pants and gave a little tug.

But there were days when Charlie would shuffle down the path like an old man. "Charlie," Roger would complain, tugging on the rope with his considerable strength, "you couldn't cross the street in a day." There were also days when, no matter how many carrots Roger offered Charlie—carrots having become his favorite snack food—he'd just stand there on the path, as inanimate as a boulder or scrub oak, and look at Roger, as if to say, "Would it be okay with you if I never moved again?" Or lower his head, his enormous nostril an inch away from some speck that had caught his olfactory attention, as if to say, "Rog, you don't mind if I spend the next eight months smelling this leaf, do you?"

Charlie was a very opinionated animal. Here's what his opinion was on any given subject: *Let's do it my way.*

Charlie wasn't totally weaned, and Roger was now the only one who could handle his antics at feeding time, the only one strong enough to hold onto the bottle when Charlie latched onto the nipple and started bunting him around. But now even Roger was having trouble. An avidly nursing four-hundred-pound baby is a different proposition from even an avidly nursing three-hundred-pound baby. Roger and Veryl had to come up with a better way to deal with Charlie's appetite. Toward the end of summer, they devised what they called "the milk bar" in the barn. They constructed a U-shaped barrier of hay bales, three high, in the barn aisle opposite Charlie's stall. Concealing the bottles behind the "bar," they would come around and open Charlie's stall door, then race frantically back behind their barricade and present the first bottle as the thirsty animal bellied up to the bar. Protected by the bales and assisted by Veryl, Roger would feed Charlie his first half-gallon bottle of goat's milk, then most of his second bottle. When there was an inch or so of milk left in the second bottle, they would come from behind the bar and lead Charlie, still polishing off bottle number two, back into his stall, then walk him back around 180 degrees so that Roger and Veryl now had their backs to the stall door, and then, at the moment Charlie drained the last drop of milk from the bottle—the moment at which Charlie would begin grunting and tap-dancing furiously for more—they would jump out of the stall. Anyone who had the opportunity to observe this precisely timed ritual was less likely in the future to refer to Charlie as "cute."

A FEW TIMES that first summer, Roger loaded Charlie into the horse trailer and hauled him up to Montosa Buffalo Ranch, two hours north of them, to have him weighed by their friend John Painter and to give him a taste of normal buffalo life. Once, the two men walked Charlie out among the herd on a lead.

"Here they are, Charlie," Roger said on one of those occasions. "Your people."

"You got *that* right," said John, who had worked with buffalo since he was a kid. "Every one of them's an individual." John wore a short graying beard, a cowboy shirt, and a feed-company gimme cap.

"No need to convince me of that," Roger replied.

"They're just like people, except they don't have opposable thumbs."

"Or language."

"Oh, they've got language, all right," John corrected him. "And don't you think they don't. Every one of those grunts means something. They're *always* jabbering to each other. And they don't miss a beat. I always know when someone's come on the ranch 'cause of how the buffalo act. They go on red alert. Hell, one cow got agitated one morning just at the sight of a goddamn hot-air balloon way off in the distance."

Half a dozen of John's buffalo edged closer to them, curious about Charlie, who showed no interest—although the difference between a buffalo showing interest and showing none may not always be apparent to the layman.

"Their reactions are so much quicker than cattle," the buffalo rancher went on, echoing Charles Goodnight's view. "And they've got big feelings, too. I had three sisters once, and when I sold off two of them, the third one was crushed. Inconsolable. Went off her feed for an entire month. Each one's got a different personality. You got your leaders and your middle-of-the-herd dwellers. I got one bull I've bonded with that I can go right up to and scratch."

Scratch? Hell, Roger thought to himself, he and Charlie were practically sleeping together.

"'Course, you got to be careful," John said, raking his fingers through his beard.

five

In the late nineteenth century, the American buffalo's survival hung by a slender thread of sentiment and serendipity. Mary Ann and Charles Goodnight, disheartened by the excesses of Man, rescued the southern herd of buffalo from extinction because they loved the animals. At almost the same time, hundreds of miles to the north, a Pend d'Oreille Indian named Samuel Walking Coyote was also starting his own herd. In his case, however, it was because he loved a woman. Actually, two of them.

In the summer of 1872, Walking Coyote left the Flathead Indian reservation in what is now northwestern Montana and traveled east across the Rockies to the Blackfeet reservation, where he spent the winter hunting buffalo with the Blackfeet Indians. There, Walking Coyote fell in love with a Blackfoot woman and married her. This would have been a more positive development in his life if he wasn't already married to a Flathead woman.

In the spring, Walking Coyote's conscience stirred and his thoughts turned to his first wife and his adopted home back on the Flathead reservation. He decided to return home—but with his new wife in tow. Only as the departure date drew near did he begin to worry about the ramifications. Flathead law forbade marrying outside the tribe. Moreover, there was a Jesuit mission on the Flathead reservation, where the Fathers would no doubt look askance at his new marital configuration.

A few days later, a solution to his predicament wandered into his hunting camp in the form of eight orphaned buffalo calves, all of them casualties of his very own buffalo hunting. The calves quickly imprinted on the Blackfoot horses, giving Walking Coyote the terrific idea of dragging the calves back over the Rockies as a peace offering to the Flatheads and the Jesuit Fathers, and possibly even to his first wife. And so it was in the spring of 1873 that he made his way with the calves back over the Rockies, losing two animals en route, but finally showing up at the Flathead Mission with six buffalo calves. The Jesuit Fathers were not charmed, and the Indian police, presumably under the Fathers' direction, thrashed him and his second wife before excommunicating Walking Coyote—probably Limping Coyote at this point—from the tribe.

He did what any self-respecting man would have done: he took his second wife and six buffalo calves and left the Flathead reservation, then made a home not far away in the Flathead Valley. Within ten years, he had thirteen buffalo—and something of a buffalo-control problem. His neighbors were not pleased. A nearby cattle rancher named Charles Allard convinced a fellow rancher and childhood friend, Michel Pablo, to offer to take the buffalo off Walking Coyote's hands for $2,000 in gold. Times had changed; as the late distinguished behavioral ecologist and buffalo expert Dale F. Lott has noted, it was probably the first time in Montana history that buffalo were worth more alive than dead. Walking Coyote agreed to the terms, took his gold, and went south to Missoula, where he went on a titanic drinking binge and eventually died broke.

But his legacy prospered under Allard and Pablo. In 1893, the two ranchers bought twenty-six more buffalo and eighteen cattalo (the offspring of buffalo bred with cattle) from C. J. "Buffalo" Jones, who had started a herd that could be traced to some buffalo calves that had survived near Winnipeg in the 1870s. Visions of profitable buffalo began stampeding in Allard and Pablo's heads. Unfortunately, Allard injured a knee that did not heal properly and, despite the attentions of surgeons in Chicago, he died in 1895 at the age of forty-three, leaving behind his partner and more than three hundred bison.

The part of Allard's share of the herd that went to his wife ended up in Kalispell, Montana, while the part belonging to the Allards' daughters and son was sold to a man who later sold fifteen of them to the U.S. government, which in 1902 decided to establish a buffalo compound in Yellowstone, the country's first national park. Yellowstone had become a haven for poachers, who hunted down most of the handful of wild buffalo that had taken refuge there during the Great Slaughter. Allard's children's fifteen buffalo, and three donated by Charles Goodnight, were shipped to Yellowstone to augment the dwindling herd whose descendants still live there today. C. J. "Buffalo" Jones, who had started his own herd with a few orphaned calves in the late 1880s, became the Park's game warden, but he was a teetotaler and his prudishness so irritated everyone that the park superintendent had to fire him.

Michel Pablo held on to his herd until 1906, when the Flathead reservation land where his six hundred buffalo grazed was opened to homesteaders. Pablo petitioned the federal government for a long-term lease on nearby public lands. While the Great Plains bison were being exterminated in the 1870s, the government had looked the other way, and even encouraged it. A generation later, Pablo now presented it with a small but golden opportunity to atone. The federal government refused. Pablo then asked the government to buy his herd from him outright. Teddy Roosevelt loved the idea, but Congress wouldn't come up with the funds, and a disgusted Pablo turned to the Canadian government for grazing rights in Alberta. The Canadians, who in 1889 had permanently banned hunting of its few hundred remaining buffalo, countered by buying his herd, paying Pablo $200 a head, only slightly more than he had paid for them twenty-two years before. Adding insult to the injury of Pablo's rejection by his own government, the ordeal of rounding up his six hundred buffalo and getting them on the train to Alberta took six long years.

There were other saviors of buffalo, notably Pete Dupree, a son of a French trapper, who captured five buffalo calves in the

Dakotas in the early 1880s. After Dupree's death, his brother-in-law sold the herd of three dozen or so animals to a Scottish immigrant named James "Scotty" Philip, who died in 1911. In 1914, Scotty Philip's sons sold thirty-six buffalo—the herd was now several hundred strong—to the state of South Dakota, where they seeded a herd that is now maintained at about 1,500 head in Custer State Park. In the 1920s the Philip sons sold off one hundred more buffalo to William Randolph Hearst for his animal preserve in San Luis Obispo, California.

American history is threaded with the stories of men who raised, admired, and often profited from the buffalo. But this scattered, uncoordinated rescue operation would not have amounted to much were it not for a naturalist and ornithologist named Ernest Harold Baynes. In 1904, he visited a game preserve in New Hampshire that boasted 160 buffalo, some of which had come from "Buffalo" Jones's Kansas ranch. Baynes had never seen buffalo before, and he was so fascinated by them that he went off on a buffalo research binge. When he learned how tenuous their existence was, he leaped into action. He wrote articles about their plight and sent letters to important people, including President Roosevelt, imploring them to take up the cause. He successfully lobbied editors to crusade for the buffalo on editorial pages, then hit the road for a lecture tour. In 1905, someone suggested that an organization devoted to the preservation of the buffalo might be a good idea. William T. Hornaday, esteemed naturalist and director of the New York Zoological Park, agreed to be the group's president, Roosevelt agreed to be honorary president, and Baynes sent a notice to two hundred bison-minded Americans for a meeting to be held on December 8, 1905, in perhaps the most unusual venue ever chosen for the founding of an organization: the lion house at the New York Zoological Park. Only fourteen of the invitees came, but it was enough to found the American Bison Society, which would devote itself to the preservation of the buffalo until it was disbanded in 1953.

The Society's first big initiative was to establish, in addition to the existing herd at Yellowstone, a new herd on a fenced federal buffalo range. It took two years, but in 1908, Congress purchased "surplus" reservation land in the Flathead Valley of western Montana, the very land where Samuel Walking Coyote had raised his calves thirty-five years before, and where Michel Pablo had grazed his herd until only recently, when he had managed to get the last of his buffalo on trains to Alberta. Since Congress had refused to come up with the funds two years earlier to buy Pablo's herd, already in the Flathead Valley, it now needed buffalo for the newly created National Bison Range. Unfortunately, Congress felt it had discharged its obligation to the buffalo by buying the land and left it to the American Bison Society to provide the animals. According to the American Bison Society's count, there were just 1,917 buffalo left in North America.

The Society solicited public donations to buy thirty-four buffalo. For many years the official story claimed melodramatically that the necessary $10,560.50 was raised by American children, one penny at a time. The reality is that four wealthy New Yorkers, including Andrew Carnegie, put up 20 percent of the total and eighty-three other New Yorkers contributed 30 percent. The remainder trickled in from the rest of the country.

Montana raised $366. Texas, North and South Dakota, and Kansas, once the heart of the American buffalo range, contributed nothing.

THE AMERICAN BISON SOCIETY struggled to re-create a remnant of a world that had been, but for the Plains Indians a way of life that had lasted thousands of years was gone forever. Since the 1880s, more and more of their meat—it was beef now, and often spoiled by the time it arrived—had come from the U.S. government. The Indians' world had been pulled out from under them. Toward the end of the Great Slaughter, Lakota (Sioux) medicine men would arrange painted buffalo skulls in a circle on the Great Plains, hoping to lure the animals back from the dead. The Indians' desperate longing for their vanished world reached fever pitch in 1889, when a young Paiute shaman named Wovoka, trained as a medicine man by his father, reported a vision of a better world that he had seen while seriously ill with a high fever. He had seen the Great Spirit, who had told him to return to his people and counsel the ways of righteousness. (He had lived for a time with a white rancher's family—where he went by the name Jack Wilson—so the overtones of Christianity were not surprising.) Wovoka returned from his trance with a new kind of ritual dance and a powerful message.

The Ghost Dance was performed for as many as four days at a time, without musical accompaniment, and it included women and children. The powerful message was this: he told them, according to twentieth-century activist and storyteller

John (Fire) Lame Deer, that "through the power of the Ghost Dance the earth would roll up like a carpet, with all the white man's works—the fences and the mining towns with their whorehouses, the factories and the farms with their stinking, unnatural animals, the railroads and the telegraph poles, the whole works. And underneath this rolled-up white man's world we could find again the flowering prairie, unspoiled, with its herds of buffalo and antelope, its clouds of birds, belonging to everyone, enjoyed by all." A world would be reborn in which the Indians and the buffalo would again rule, in which the Indian dead would return, and all would live in peace and prosperity. "Listen, he said, yonder the buffalo are coming," went one of the Ghost Dance religion's songs, "The Buffalo Are Coming." "These are his sayings, yonder the buffalo are coming / They walk, they stand, they are coming / Yonder the buffalo are coming."

The gospel, and the dancing, spread through the reservations. Into the summer of 1890, the Ghost Dance continued to gather up the frustrations of the Indian peoples and vent it in mass frenzies. Then, barely a year and a half since Wovoka had emerged from his fever with a new religion, some nervous Indian agents on the Sioux reservation in Pine Ridge, South Dakota, banned it among their six thousand charges. But the dancing continued, and fears mounted among the Indian agents and other government officials, some of whom were afraid that the Ghost Dance was in reality a war dance that would lead to riots. The tensions led finally to the murder of Sitting Bull and eight Sioux warriors on December 15, 1890, and, two weeks later, to the butchering of more than two hundred Indians at

Wounded Knee Creek in South Dakota. The men who did it were with the U.S. Seventh Cavalry—the same doomed unit that General George Custer had led at the Battle of Little Bighorn fourteen years earlier.

"I did not know then how much was ended," Black Elk wrote of the massacre forty years later. "When I look back now from this high hill of my old age, I can still see the butchered women and children lying heaped and scattered all along the crooked gulch as plain as when I saw them with eyes young. And I can see that something else died there in the bloody mud, and was buried in the blizzard. A people's dream died there. It was a beautiful dream . . . the nation's hoop is broken and scattered. There is no center any longer, and the sacred tree is dead."

But the symbolic buffalo was indestructible. According to Lakota legend, twenty generations ago the White Buffalo Calf Woman visited the Lakota people, taught them sacred ceremonies, and told them she would return one day in their time of need, her arrival heralded by the birth of a white buffalo calf. In 1996, near the site of the massacre at Wounded Knee 106 years before, a rare white calf named Medicine Wheel was born to a buffalo owned by Joe Merrival on the Lakota's Pine Ridge Reservation in South Dakota, in the single poorest county in America. "For us," Lakota indian Floyd Hand Looks For Buffalo said at the time, "this would be something like coming to see Jesus lying in the manger." But when Medicine Wheel, his hide now turned dark, was approaching the age of four, he escaped from his enclosure, wandered into a road, allegedly charged some vehicles, and was shot to death by a tribal member, at the request of a police officer, "for the safety of the community."

Two years earlier, in 1994, another white buffalo calf named Miracle was born on the ranch of Dave Heider in Janesville, Wisconsin. Miracle too was regarded as a messiah, and before passing away attracted so many visitors—as many as 2,500 people a day—that Heider had to build a parking lot next to his Janesville farmhouse to accommodate the tourists. "I see what Miracle does to and for other people," he said when the buffalo was a few years old. "I've seen everything from people who go weak in the knees and fall down on all fours to people standing and weeping."

six

July turned to August, and Charlie became a bigger and bigger part of Roger and Veryl's life—in fact, about two pounds bigger every day. Like most animals, buffalo grow from childhood to adolescence without much fanfare, and although Charlie would not reach his full adult size until he was three, Roger was now busy trying to negotiate the new balance of power between them. This was something with which Roger had fairly extensive experience, having flown for the Central Intelligence Agency, toiled on behalf of a pilots' union, and negotiated with art collectors, among other activities in which a judicious blend of persuasion and humility is a distinct advantage.

Buffalo people have a saying: "Find out where the buffalo

wants to be and then put the fence around him." Roger knew the limits of his power with Charlie; he could dominate him only to the extent that it would make him reasonably safe to handle. He knew that Charlie would recognize and resent any further attempt at control, and might possibly, being hardwired to act like the unneutered buffalo he was, decide to attack him. On the other hand, if he indulged Charlie too much, he ran the risk of appearing to be just another calf that Charlie, however innocently, could bat around with impunity. Any extremity in his method would backfire. There was only one tool that worked—neither force nor ingratiation, but the same kind of steady, gentle pressure that can occasionally gain an important concession from management or even be used to successfully train a teenager, over a period of years, to hang up wet towels.

One of Roger's best tools was the trick of redirecting Charlie's natural aggression to similarly sized objects other than himself, in particular a fifty-five-gallon plastic drum that soon became Charlie's favorite sparring partner. In the wild, at this age, Charlie would be jousting with fellow calves and even testing his aggression with an indulgent bull bison or two, so he probably had no greater joy by late summer than being wrestled with and cuffed lightly about the head and neck by his best friend Roger, who always kept the drum handy for surrogate duty when Charlie's excitement got the better of him. Roger also had another trick: he'd leave Charlie alone altogether after dusk, when buffalo are most dangerous.

Roger tried not to dwell on the fact it would soon be time to pack Charlie up and take him back to Montana. He had encouraged Veryl to get a bison calf in the first place, for her art, the business that supported them, but Charlie had brought something lasting into his life—a potent mix of excitement, concern, danger, and companionship—that Roger hadn't noticed he was missing. He wondered whether, by sheer chance, and despite the U.S. Department of the Interior's Wildlife Leaflet 212, he might be the temporary custodian of one of those rare wild animals with a genuine capacity for interacting with people. Charlie had more of that capacity than most *people* Roger knew.

One afternoon in August, Roger was wrestling with Charlie in the arena—"Whatcha gonna do about that?" he chided as he stiff-armed Charlie's brow, then took his head between his hands and playfully jerked it back and forth, saying, "Now whatcha gonna do about *that?*"—when he saw Veryl walking down the path from the house holding a cordless phone.

"It's Doris," she called out—Doris Breinholt, who, with her husband, managed the Medicine Lodge Buffalo Ranch in Montana.

Seeing Veryl smiling at him in her sandals, jeans, and CANDY KITCHEN WOLF REFUGE T-shirt, he smiled too. He had had a lot of luck in his life—coming home from Laos in one piece, for instance—but nothing to compare with falling in love with Veryl Goodnight and having her fall in love with him.

"C'mon, Charlie," he said, turning toward the far end of the arena, where Veryl was standing at the fence chatting on the phone with Doris. "Come say hello." Charlie fell into a trot beside him.

At the fence, Roger took the phone while Charlie stuck his head between the fence rails and began blissfully sucking on Veryl's hand.

"Hi, Doris," Roger said.

"How's my boy?" asked Doris.

"Your boy's terrific. You know, I think he's finally forgiven us for kicking him out of the house. I've just been in the arena doing my best impression of a bison calf so he has someone to play with."

"I know he's going to be disappointed when he discovers that real buffalo don't wear blue jeans."

"Or have thinning hair," Roger said. "I guess you're wondering when you're getting him back."

"Well, that's the thing. That's why I'm calling. We've got a big construction project going on right now, and Stuart and I just don't have the time to be bottle-feeding him, so I was wondering whether you'd mind holding on to him until he's weaned. Shouldn't be more than another month or so."

"Mind?" Roger said, throwing a big smile in Veryl's direction. "Doris, I'd be delighted."

"Not too much trouble?"

"Doris, I don't know what Veryl told you, but this is an extraordinary animal and we're going to miss him when he's gone."

"All right then. Just give Stuart or me a call when he's ready."

∾

ROGER KNEW BETTER than to read too much into an animal's behavior, but it did seem that Charlie was showing his appreciation for the extended stay. He always grunted softly now when Roger came down to the pen, tossed his head lightly when Roger stroked the top of his wide muzzle, and trotted more happily after him when Roger went up to the gate to get the mail. One September Sunday morning, Charlie, who still had yard privileges much of the time, was patrolling the grounds, inflicting minor damage as usual to flowers and shrubs. Roger, who was reading the Sunday papers in a lawn chair under a cloudless sky, suddenly felt hot buffalo breath in his ear. Charlie had quietly stolen up on him, in the same surreptitious manner that a herd of buffalo you might be watching in the distance would suddenly, and without your being able to say exactly how, be two hundred yards closer to you.

"Hey," Roger said, scratching Charlie under the eye. Charlie responded by ducking his head and rubbing the side of his head against Roger's leg. It was as if he didn't want to let go of his childhood among humans, even as his deepest nature stirred within him.

A somewhat disturbing idea began to occur to Roger and Veryl. They began to consider the possibility that Charlie, the proud descendant of so many generations of noble buffalo, who was acting more and more like a buffalo with every passing day, had no idea at all that he was, in fact, a buffalo. After all, though Charlie was hardly the first bison to be hand-raised, he was perhaps the first to be hand-raised in an environment that didn't contain any other buffalo. Even Charles and Mary Ann

Goodnight's first two calves had each other for company. Most, if not all, orphaned buffalo calves had been hand-raised at buffalo ranches where they saw, related with, and were eventually reintroduced to their own kind. Charlie, on the other hand, saw other buffalo only on occasional excursions to the Montosa, where he had no desire to interact with them and didn't appear to consider them as objects worthy even of his curiosity.

"He's only known the company of dogs, cats, horses, and humans," Roger said to Veryl one afternoon as they watched him wallow in a dusty patch of the arena.

"And the cats don't really count," Veryl replied. "I don't know if he's ever noticed them at all. Maybe he thinks he's a large dog."

"Or possibly an extremely hairy human being," Roger suggested. "Who knows what's going through that huge bison head of his?" That it didn't seem to have crossed Charlie's mind that he was a buffalo was a somewhat troubling irony for a couple who had never thought for a moment that Charlie was anything *but* a buffalo, and who prided themselves on their respect for any animal's integrity.

By late September, Charlie was virtually weaned. Roger's mood darkened a bit at the idea of Charlie's imminent return to Idaho at precisely the moment when Roger could retire from the job of feeding him. He tried to console himself with the thought that before long Charlie would at last have the chance to discover his buffalo-ness.

"How's that construction project going?" Roger asked when Marlo called him in early October.

"Just fine. Just fine, Roger. Doris and Stuart say they're

ready to take Charlie off your hands whenever you can get him up here."

"Uh, Marlo?"

"Yes, Roger."

"I just realized something."

"What's that?"

"Well, Charlie's too big to fit into my plane."

"You could always take another seat out."

"I still don't think I can cram him in, Marlo."

"Well, it's an awfully long drive."

"I could always wait until spring and then throw him in the horse trailer."

Marlo paused for a moment on the other end of the line. "Well, it's fine with me. As long as he's not too much of a handful, Roger."

"No, he's not trouble. I've even grown kind of fond of him."

"So I've gathered. But, listen, Roger, I know you're a talented horseman and a great lover of animals in general, but we're talking about a growing buffalo. Don't make the mistake of getting so wrapped up in him that you forget what you're dealing with."

"I spent ten years in the pilots' union fighting the FAA and the airlines for better air safety and lived to tell the tale. I've got to believe I can keep myself from getting gored by a bison."

seven

A week or so later, Roger was at his desk when the phone rang. The moment he heard Marlo Goble's voice, his heart sank. Maybe Marlo had changed his mind about Charlie. In the several days since they'd spoken, Roger had allowed himself to acknowledge his true feelings for Charlie. He had added Charlie to the short list of animals he had truly loved in his life, a list that basically contained his horse Kepler and a cat named Ace, who had kept him company during many of his bachelor years.

"Roger," Marlo said, "I've been thinking."

Here it comes.

"I've been thinking that it doesn't make any sense for you to drive a yearling buffalo up here next spring, especially when you're already so darned attached, and by next spring the two of you will probably be engaged. Why don't you just hold on to him?"

"Hold on to him for how long?"

"As long as you like."

"As long as I like? You wouldn't mind?"

"I've got plenty of bison. Consider it an early Christmas present."

"Thank you, Marlo. *Thank* you."

After he hung up, Roger strode around the corner to the doorway to Veryl's studio and announced, "Honey, I'm a rich man."

Veryl's first thought was that the stock market had rebounded. "What happened?"

"Marlo just called. And he's giving us Charlie!" Roger beamed.

"Fantastic," Veryl said, trying unsuccessfully to match her husband's enthusiasm.

"What did you tell him?"

"I told him, 'Thank you!' "

"Fantastic." But Veryl was thinking: we can't do this! We can't have a buffalo living with us on the outskirts of Santa Fe! We don't have enough grass on our property, our trees and shrubs deserve better, our PVC horse fencing isn't strong enough, and who knows how long Roger can handle him? She knew it was a losing battle, though; a man's passions were rarer and deeper as he aged and she'd never deprive Roger of his newest one.

In the next few weeks, Veryl's concerns, rather than Roger's optimism, more accurately mirrored reality. Roger was the only one who could physically handle Charlie, so all Charlie-related chores now fell to him. Roger's world was increasingly defined by the buffalo. Charlie was a rapidly growing responsibility in every sense, and with every new pound of weight and quarter-inch of horn, he became a bigger threat to Roger's carefully maintained balance of power. There were evenings when Charlie, his tail standing straight up, stood glowering at the plastic drum, about to do battle, and Roger knew better than even to enter the arena. Charlie's testosterone levels would soon be spiking, but for Roger and Veryl, on principle, neutering was out of the question because he was going to be released into a herd. In fact, Roger often thought about how he would some-day visit the herd, spot Charlie in the distance, and think, "That's my buffalo."

Veryl, more preoccupied with the bronze, not the real, version of Charlie, kept her mouth shut, but by mid-November, spring was looking mighty far away to Roger. He reluctantly came to the conclusion that the initial plan—to let Charlie be a buffalo among buffalo—now made practical as well as every other kind of sense.

Roger didn't want to send Charlie back to Marlo Goble's ranch, where he would face an uncertain fate. Instead, he called John Painter—Charlie's "Uncle John," as he had come to be known around the house. John knew Charlie, his ranch was only two hours away, and he treated his bison with a love and respect that, although no match for Roger's buffalo sentiments, was unusual.

"I'd be happy to have him," Painter said.

"I'm going to pay you a boarding fee, John, 'cause I don't want anything to happen to him."

"Heck, Roger, you know I'd never let anything happen to ol' Charlie."

"I wish I could hold on to him myself, but some things are just bigger than we are."

"A buffalo would be one of them."

"I tried."

"Roger, I'd say you've gone where few men have dared to go. If I didn't know you better, I'd say you were a softhearted old sentimentalist with a crush on an ungulate."

"It's more than that, John. Buffalo are like the ghosts of American history. Being with Charlie's like touching the past."

"Okay, so you're a softhearted old *poet* with a crush on an ungulate."

IT TOOK ROGER a couple of weeks to break the news to Charlie. They were taking one of their walks down the arroyo on their property as a light December snow fell, dusting the piñon pine and small prickly-pear cactuses.

"It's like this, Charlie," he said, "and I don't want to get all emotional about it, so don't make it any harder on me than it has to be." He cleared his throat. "Veryl and I think it's time for you to learn how to be a buffalo. Now, what do you think of that?"

Charlie, who now came up to Roger's waist, pushed his wet nose up against Roger's behind and butted him down the path. It was a little like being nudged by a small snowplow.

"Here's the thing," Roger said when they got to the bottom of the rise, "we've had a lot of great times together. Just about as much fun as a couple of people and a buffalo can have."

Charlie snorted two little clouds of condensation.

Roger laid his hand on top of Charlie's head as they walked along side by side. "If you weren't so big, this might not be an issue. Of course, if you weren't so darn big you wouldn't be a buffalo, which is one of the things I like about you. But you are. You already weigh over four hundred pounds, and before it's all over, you're going to weigh two *thousand* pounds. Don't take this the wrong way, but I've owned cars that weigh less than that."

They walked on a bit while Roger tried to think of a way to put a more positive spin on it.

"Listen," he said, "pretty soon you're not going to want to hang out anymore with Luke and Mickey and Veryl and me. You're going to want to hang out with other two-thousand-pound animals. I'm talking bison."

Charlie stopped to inspect some dead leaves lying in the arroyo.

"It's time for you to be what you are," Roger said, surprised that his eyes were getting a little misty. "And that's a buffalo."

Veryl and Roger decided to have a big going-away party for Charlie in mid-December and invite the people who had been part of his life. The guest list included Veryl's eighty-three-year-old Uncle Dean Goodnight from Phoenix, Dr. Marlo Goble and his wife Michele from Medicine Lodge, and a cousin of Veryl's from Lubbock, Texas, named Andy Wilkinson, a singer/songwriter/English professor/ex-cop, whose great-great-grandmother had been Charles Goodnight's sister. Andy had recorded a number of CDs, including several very moving songs about Charles and Mary Ann Goodnight, the extermination of the buffalo, Goodnight's old friend Chief Quanah Parker of the Comanches, and life on the plains and the Texas Panhandle.

On the morning of the get-together, Roger was out in the yard helping get things ready when he had a run-in with Charlie that helped him overcome some of his guilt about giving him up. The weather was now cold enough that Roger was on his hands and knees on the patio, struggling to plug in the electrical cord for the heated cat bed, when he felt some light pressure against one hip, then another, followed quickly by a vise-like sensation on either side of his waist. As Charlie briefly pounded Roger's skull against the wall of the house, Roger braced himself against the wall, finally summoning the strength to raise his torso and force Charlie off his back.

When Roger appeared a few moments later in the kitchen, where Veryl was overseeing the caterer, he brushed a few leaves off his jeans and said, "Honey, I just want you to know that I'm trying as hard as I can to be faithful to you, but it's getting to be a challenge."

"Don't tell me," Veryl said, a smile breaking across her face.

"I was on my hands and knees out there and I had a visitor. At least the cat bed's all plugged in."

"And was it good for you?"

"Let's just say that his technique left something to be desired."

THE CHRISTMAS/FAREWELL-TO-CHARLIE PARTY went off without any further hitches. Late in the evening, the sixty or so guests took seats in Veryl's studio and the white-bearded, cowboy-hatted Andy Wilkinson pulled out his acoustic guitar and sang a new song, "Blood on the Bison," that he had written as a companion piece to "Back from the Brink," the sculpture for which Charlie had modeled.

Marlo unveiled the first casting of "Back from the Brink" and everyone applauded emotionally. The bronze portrayed Mary Ann Goodnight nursing one hungry calf while the second pressed against her body. Mary Ann looked off into the distance, as though scanning the horizon for any threat to the precious lives that were now her responsibility. While Andy performed a second song, "A Prairie Without Buffalo," Roger snuck out of the house. A few minutes later, as Andy sang the refrain—

Only in your dreams you'll know
The world we should have saved
For the prairie without buffalo
Is the ocean without waves.

—the side door of the studio opened. Through it, Roger appeared, quickly followed by Charlie on a lead. There were several gasps as Roger led him over to Andy, where Charlie stood, facing the guests, as Andy finished his song. Then the whole room burst into applause.

THREE WEEKS LATER, on January 2, 2001, Roger and Veryl loaded Charlie into the horse trailer and drove him up to John Painter's Montosa Buffalo Ranch near Taos, New Mexico, to introduce him to a couple of buffalo his own age. Buffalo University, they kept calling it.

"It's time to make an honest bison out of you," Roger said when they arrived at the ranch and he opened the door of the trailer. Roger and John Painter led Charlie down the aluminum ramp.

Veryl let Charlie suck on her hand for a minute or two, just like she used to when she was weaning him from the bottle. "Thanks for being such a wonderful part of the family," she whispered.

"We're going to miss you, Charlie," Roger said, "even if the next time you see us, all you're thinking about is teenage buffalo cows." But his jokes couldn't hide his sorrow, especially from himself.

Roger and John Painter led him into the pen, which was surrounded by a heavy steel buffalo-proof fence and contained two other seven-month-old buffalo, a male and a female, who stood together in the middle of the corral, eyeing the proceedings. When the men left the pen and closed the gate behind them, Charlie stood quite still with his back to the humans, studying the other buffalo, with no idea of what to do.

"Go on, Charlie," Roger called out, "they won't bite."

"Remember, Charlie," Veryl said, "you're a *buffalo*."

"Come on, son," Roger said. "Go say hello to your new friends."

Charlie finally moved, but not toward the buffalo. He walked sadly to a corner of the pen, as far away from the other animals as possible, and hung his head.

The other two bison watched him for another minute, then turned and shambled to the far end. If Charlie had been a kindergartner, Roger or Veryl would have taken him by the hand and showed him there was nothing to be afraid of, but all they could do was make their way back to the trailer for the drive home to Santa Fe. No other buffalo in the history of the world had ever taken so many naps and hikes with a human being. It wasn't easy for Roger and Veryl, who didn't have human children and were getting on a bit themselves, to give up Charlie after nursing and caring for him from the time he was just a week old, and then watching him become a genuine member of their family. But it was no less true of animals than it was of humans that, if you loved them enough, you sometimes had to let them leave.

As they pulled away from the Montosa Buffalo Ranch, they didn't look back. They knew that if they did, they would see Charlie watching them go.

eight

That night, Roger and Veryl sat in their living room in front of a crackling fire. "Listen to this," Veryl said, looking up from her newspaper. "Some rancher in Oregon got in trouble with the law and abandoned his herd of buffalo. So they wandered onto an Indian reservation and now no one can figure out how to round them up. The Indians set a trap for them, thinking they might start their own herd, but the buffalo are too smart to fall for it. They're fast learners."

"Well, you're either a fast learner or a buffalo burger," Roger muttered from behind his book.

"Now that's a pleasant thought," she said. "It's bad enough

having Charlie gone without thinking of him as somebody's lunch."

Roger put down the book, which he had only been pretending to read. "Kind of quiet without him."

"He never made all that much noise in the first place."

"Okay, but just knowing he's not outside in his pen makes me feel a little lonely."

"We'll get used to it," Veryl said.

"Not half as fast as I got used to that prairie dog of yours being gone."

Veryl looked ceilingward. "I hope you're happy, Petey, wherever you are. And you, too, Calamity Coyote."

Calamity was an abandoned coyote she had taken in for a while back in Colorado, before Roger's time. "She was no Petey," Veryl said now. "And a far, far cry from Charlie. She wouldn't bond, not even when I tried to lure her into bed by putting chicken bones under the blankets."

"Thanks for not trying that with me."

"Believe me, you didn't need chicken bones. But with Calamity, nothing worked. That's why I called her Calamity Coyote. It was like a very long, bad date. When she was finally old enough to be released, I took her to a clearing at the edge of the forest and she took off like a shot toward the trees."

"She couldn't wait to get away from the damn chicken bones."

"But just before disappearing, she pulled up, turned, and looked back at me. It was more eye contact than we'd had in a long time. Then the most peculiar thing happened: after a moment, she ran back and jumped into my arms for a huge hug, something she hadn't wanted in all the months she was with me. We hugged for maybe fifteen seconds and then I put her down and she took off for good."

"Like Houdini," Roger said. At the request of the New Mexico Game and Fish Department, he and Veryl had wintered a lost black bear cub some years earlier after a severe drought had driven a lot of wildlife down into Santa Fe looking for food. They kept her in the barn's one empty stall—later to be occupied by Charlie—which they thought they had made escape-proof. But the cub found a way out, earning her name, and was recaptured in the same spot in downtown Santa Fe, ten miles away, where she had gone looking for her mother. Following a tightening of barn security, Houdini remained with them throughout the winter, living the life of a caged but well-fed wild animal. Roger and Veryl kept their distance, knowing that the only way to ensure her survival in the future was to make sure she did *not* learn to like people. If she did, she would gravitate toward them, become a problem, and eventually get shot. Roger and Veryl's goal was to provide her with only basic care and release her in the spring. When the time came, they called the Game and Fish Department, who sent out a warden to tranquilize her with a dart gun. Then they put her in an animal transporter, a truck whose back half was an enclosure, and drove her to a release area a few hours away.

At their destination, they let Houdini settle in her cage for a little while. Before he finally opened the door for her, Roger had his hand resting against the steel mesh when Houdini, now recovered from the tranquilizer and fully aware, came over and rested her nose against his knuckle. It was the first time she had shown him anything other than contempt. Now the bear kept her nose against his hand for a full minute. Whether it was to acknowledge that she knew she hadn't been the easiest animal to live with, or simply in gratitude for being allowed to go, Roger would never know.

"Well, at least things can get back to normal," he said to Veryl now. There was a part of him, of course, that was relieved that Charlie had found a home. They had done their job, and it had only been Charlie's freakishly friendly personality that made his departure so hard. Roger was actually eager to get on with his life, even if in his heart he knew that "normal" had changed a few months ago. "Normal" had become life with Charlie.

That night, Roger lay in bed, listening to the coyotes and trying to fall asleep.

"You awake?" he whispered to Veryl in the dark.

"Yeah."

"This is hard."

"I know," she said. It reminded her of the childhood sadness of watching her beloved snow horses melt every spring.

VERY EARLY THE NEXT MORNING, the phone rang. It was John Painter.

"Hey, John," Roger said, looking at the clock. It wasn't even six yet. "What's up?"

"I'm sorry to call at this hour, Roger, but I think you need to get over here."

"What's going on?"

"Charlie's down and he can't get up."

"What?!" Roger felt like he'd been hit over the head. "What happened?"

"I don't know, but he's down by one of the fence posts and he can't get up. He might've run headlong into it. Maybe you'd better get over here soon as you can."

Roger woke up Veryl, and they jumped into their clothes and hitched the horse trailer back up to the Chevy Tahoe, in case they had to get Charlie to a doctor. They threw Mickey and Luke in the truck with them and started the two-hour drive to the ranch just as the sun broke over the horizon. Every mile was torture for them. Roger felt sick. He knew that angry or frightened buffalo sometimes charged blindly into walls, barns, fences. Charlie had probably panicked. To an animal who had never been with his own kind, two other buffalo probably seemed like a crowd. Maybe one of them had picked a fight and Charlie had run away as fast as he could—right into the fence. All of John Painter's fencing was steel well-pipe fencing—strong enough to stop any buffalo. Behind the wheel, Roger winced with second thoughts. What had he been thinking, leaving Charlie there? He didn't know what he would be facing when he arrived—whether Charlie had just had his bell rung or whether Roger might have to . . . well, he didn't even want to complete the thought.

Roger floored the Tahoe all the way there—more, it would turn out later, than the transmission could actually bear. Mile after mile of desert and incongruous garish Indian casinos sped silently by, bathed in dawn's pink light. When Roger and Veryl finally reached Montosa Buffalo Ranch and climbed down from the overheated truck, the frigid January air hit them like a slap in the face. They saw John Painter crouching by Charlie just inside the pen at the foot of a steel fence post. Because it's dangerous for big animals, especially ruminants, to be on their sides for too long, John had him lying sternal, propped up on either side with hay bales. As Veryl and Roger approached, they saw a trickle of blood running out of Charlie's right nostril. His right eye was bloodshot and rolled back. As soon as the two of them climbed inside the pen and crouched next to him, Charlie greeted them with a low, sorrowful grunt.

"Hi," Veryl said.

"Charlie," Roger said.

"The vet's been here already," John said, petting Charlie's head with a gloved hand. "Gave him steroids to stop any swelling around his spinal cord. But he hasn't moved since we found him this way this morning. We put hay and water in front of him, but he won't touch it." After this brief medical report, John, who was closer to Charlie than anyone besides Roger and Veryl, lost his composure. "Jesus," he said with a grimace. "Any buffalo but Charlie."

"Charlie," Veryl whispered as she stroked his face. "What happened?" She offered him her ungloved hand, and he weakly sucked it.

John said, "It's pretty obvious he ran headlong into this post."

"Let's hope he's just knocked himself silly," Roger said. "Let's hope he gets up."

But he didn't get up. John put them up in the ranch house, and for the next two very cold days and freezing nights, Roger and Veryl took turns staying with Charlie, snuggling up to keep him warm. At night, under a navy blue field of stars and a pile of warm blankets, they soothed and encouraged him, hoping for some improvement. But all they got were mournful, heart-rending, please-don't-leave-me grunts from Charlie whenever one of them went back to the house to warm up. On the third day, Ray Loretto, the first Indian veterinarian in New Mexico, came by, watched Charlie at last try to get up, and concluded that he had dislocated his left shoulder. Loretto rolled Charlie over onto his right side, climbed on top, and popped the joint back into place. But Charlie still couldn't move on his own. Mickey licked his cheek.

On the third day, Roger, Veryl, and John agreed they couldn't wait around helplessly anymore for Charlie to live or die. Roger called the one place he figured could help Charlie now—the School of Veterinary Medicine at Colorado State University, 375 miles away. When Roger told Dr. Shelley Sandberg from the Food Animal Department that he had a paralyzed seven-month-old buffalo who needed help, she told him to drive on up. She said they treated mostly cattle, not many buffalo (and even that turned out to be a gross overstatement)—but that she'd be waiting for them.

So Roger and three ranch hands loaded 450 pounds of dead weight named Charlie into the horse trailer.

"We saved him once," Veryl said as they pulled away from the Montosa Buffalo Ranch. "Okay, so we'll save him again."

The road was endless, a black line of bad thoughts. Roger kept calling the school from his cell phone to remind them they were on their way. He imagined the whole staff waiting and waiting, then giving up before they arrived. Finally, late on Friday night, after seven long hours, Roger and Veryl pulled up to the entrance of a barnlike building at Colorado State University's School of Veterinary Medicine. Roger got out and banged on the door. When it opened, five young women came out—Dr. Shelley Sandberg and four veterinary graduate students. Two of them were pushing a big gurney—a stretcher on wheels just a few inches off the ground.

"I'm not sure we have enough manpower," Roger said. Not one of the young women was even as big as Veryl. "There's no way the five of you and us are going to be able to pick Charlie up."

Dr. Sandberg squared her shoulders and said, "It's ten-thirty on Friday night. What you see is what you get. What do you say we get the animal on the gurney?"

With a little help from Roger and Veryl, the five women managed to move Charlie from the horse trailer onto the gurney and wheel him into a stall that had already been prepared. It was covered with sand for better traction—not that Charlie looked like he was going to be on his feet anytime soon. While Veryl and Roger looked on, Dr. Sandberg examined Charlie. She took a long needle and stuck it into one of Charlie's hind legs. The leg twitched. "Good boy," she whispered to him. She repeated the procedure on his other three legs. Each time Charlie twitched.

"Good," Sandberg said. "His spinal cord's not severed."

The students fed the straps of a bright blue sling under Charlie's belly, a switch was thrown, and an electric hoist slowly raised him to a standing position. The sling was attached to a track running along the barn ceiling in order to support an injured animal learning to walk again. Roger and Veryl were shocked when the little engine stopped. Charlie's legs just dangled, brushing the floor. He hung there, like the world's largest puppet between shows.

For the next two days, Charlie lay on a bed of straw for two hours at a time until some of the graduate students came in and hoisted him in his sling for an hour or two, hoping his brain would remember how to make his legs walk. Two hours on the straw, two hours in the hoist. Over and over again. Veryl and Roger had taken a room in a nearby hotel, and each time Charlie was in the sling, they came to help. Roger took hold of Charlie's front legs, Veryl took hold of his back ones, and they moved them in a walking motion. Charlie's legs, which had only days before been chasing Roger around the arena, never moved on their own.

On Monday, while Veryl and Roger were rubbing Charlie as he lay in his stall, a slim, balding man in his mid-forties approached them. "I'm Dr. Rob Callan," he said, shaking their hands. "Professor of Food Animal Medicine and Surgery. Dr. Sandberg's told me all about Charlie." He looked down at the motionless buffalo. "She says you've got a pretty special bison."

"We've hand-raised him since he was a week old," Roger said. "We want to do whatever we can."

"I don't care what it takes," Veryl said. "Make him walk again."

Callan nodded—a barely perceptible, meditative nod. "Well, we'll certainly do everything we can, but I want to be honest with you about his chances." He glanced at Charlie again. "Maybe we should step outside."

Roger laid a hand on Charlie's head. "We'll be right back," he said, and the doctor led them through the double doors into the hallway.

nine

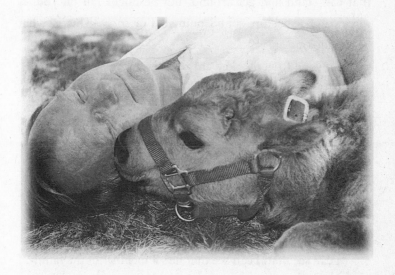

"Here's how it is." Callan spoke very slowly, making Veryl and Roger even more anxious. "Charlie must have hit that fence going full-out, because he's clearly suffered a serious neck injury and trauma to his spinal cord and it's affected his nerves. We grade neurologic injuries from one to five. Five's the worst. The animal's down and can't get up. That's Charlie. He's a five."

"A five," Veryl repeated.

"In the best cases—the *very* best cases—you get two grades of improvement. Maximum. For Charlie, that means he could get to a three."

Veryl waited for Roger to ask, but he didn't, so she had to. "A three?"

Callan spoke behind steepled fingers. "A three's an animal that can stand and get around, but he might fall on you. A three's not a pasture-sound animal. I'm sorry. This is what you're looking at."

Veryl and Roger looked at the floor.

"More often than not—" he paused again. "More often than not, they don't stand up again."

Veryl covered her mouth with her hand. Roger just stared at Callan.

"I believe in being straight with people," Dr. Callan said. "Of course, most of our experience comes from horses and cattle. And you never know."

"Charlie's not your average animal," Roger said.

"I can see that. I can see that he's a member of the family. I don't underestimate the role that love can play. Also, I know from Dr. Sandberg how cooperative Charlie is. He tolerates a lot of handling. To see that in a bison is exceptional. He seems to understand that we're trying to help him. That's a big, big plus."

"He's known nothing but love," Veryl said.

"And it shows. All right, the first thing you have to do is make a decision about Charlie's care. I'd like to X-ray his neck and take a myelogram."

"Remind me what that is," Roger said.

"We shoot some dye into the spinal fluid and see what's going on in there. Among other things, it allows us to see how bad the swelling is pressing on the spinal cord."

"Whatever it takes," Veryl said, holding Roger's hand tightly.

"There's just one problem," Dr. Callan said.

More problems? Roger thought.

"We have to anesthetize Charlie to do the procedure, and there's a risk with ruminants. From our limited experience, we know in general they seem to have problems with anesthesia. A small percentage regurgitate when given anesthesia and they aspirate the contents of their stomach. And they suffocate. One in a hundred," Callan said. "At worst, one in ten."

Well, which was it? Roger thought. One in a hundred or one in ten? But he knew it didn't matter. They were either going to do what they could for Charlie, or they weren't.

"If there's something wrong that we can repair and we *don't* know about it," Callan continued, "and Charlie doesn't get better on his own, you could lose him, anyway."

Veryl and Roger glanced at each other.

"I should tell you something else," Callan added. "I've never worked on a buffalo before."

"No?" Veryl said.

"We've never had a buffalo admitted here. But a spinal column's a spinal column." He smiled, trying to relieve the terrible tension. "I'll give you a few minutes to think it over."

Callan disappeared down the corridor and Roger and Veryl sat down on chairs in the corner.

Roger said, "If Charlie dies from the drugs needed to keep him quiet enough for an X-ray and a myelogram, we'll never know if he might have gotten well all by himself."

"But according to Dr. Callan," Veryl said, "he's not much of a candidate for getting better on his own. He's a five, Roger. Dr. Callan was pretty clear—fives rarely get up on their feet again. You know if this were any other animal, if we were more practical people, we'd have to put him down. If we don't let Dr. Callan put Charlie under and find out exactly what's going on, and he doesn't get well on his own, we'll hate ourselves for not giving the doctors a chance to save him."

"I know you're right," Roger finally said. "And I'd rather make the decision to do something instead of nothing."

"So we'll let him go ahead?"

"We've got to."

An hour later, he and Veryl watched as the doctors put a line in a vein in Charlie's leg and put him quickly under. Then the surgical team put a ventilator down Charlie's throat to help him breathe, and Dr. Callan asked Roger and Veryl to leave the operating room. On her way out, Veryl stopped and whispered in Callan's ear, "Please save Charlie, Doc. Next to me, he's Roger's best friend."

They had two hours. Veryl suggested they go out and shop. Walk around. Something. Anything. Roger said no. He just wanted to sit there, staring silently into space. Waiting. Thinking. Until seven months ago, he had never seen a bison or even given them much thought. Now he was taking extraordinary measures to save one buffalo's life. He sensed that, if Charlie survived, their lives would forever be linked.

ROGER HAD NEVER DONE things lightly. His first passion was flying. At twenty-one, he indulged a childhood dream by taking lessons, even though it was a tremendous financial drain. He worked construction jobs to pay for it. Impressed by Roger's natural gift for aviation, his first instructor suggested a career as a pilot, but Roger had already entered a corporate training program as an Arizona State undergraduate. By the time he was out of college, he was already disenchanted with corporate America and spent most of his waking hours at airports, chasing airplanes, begging for a chance to be somebody's copilot. He scrimped and saved to get his private and commercial licenses, his instrument and multi-engine ratings.

He had everything but a job, and then a friend mentioned a small ad she had seen in a Phoenix newspaper for contract flying in Southeast Asia. It was the spring of 1968, only a few months after the Tet Offensive, so Roger knew what "contract flying in Southeast Asia" probably meant, but he was antsy about getting his career off the ground. He applied for the job, flying to Washington, D.C., for the interview. The job entailed flying relief missions to refugees in a DC-3. He suspected otherwise, but said nothing. He was examined and tested.

His Phoenix flying instructor had been right about his skills; of five thousand applicants, sixteen were hired and Roger Brooks was the youngest member of the crop. He became a pilot for Air America, the clandestine arm of the CIA whose roots were as a private guerrilla airline hauling cargo in post–World War II China. By the late 1960s, Air America was in the business of serving "national security interests" in Asia. At one point during the Vietnam War, Air America would have the third-largest airline fleet in the world, logging as many as thirty thousand flights a month. Roger Brooks's dream had come true, and then some; he had one of the riskiest jobs in all of aviation.

While the war in Vietnam was tearing both that country and America apart, the CIA was waging a secret war in Laos to help General Vang Pao's army fight a Communist takeover there by destroying its supply line, the Ho Chi Minh Trail. Along with hundreds of other civilian pilots, Roger had been recruited for a military operation whose existence the U.S. government flatly denied. The work included hauling mercenaries and ammunition deep into Laos, rescuing downed pilots, running resupply missions, doing photo reconnaissance, evacuating endangered locals, and making humanitarian food drops.

Roger flew night orbits over the Ho Chi Minh Trail, communicating with road watch teams whose job was to spot enemy truck and troop traffic coming down the Trail. He flew an unpressurized plane at twenty thousand feet, just clearing the effective range of most antiaircraft guns, but he still felt like a mallard on the opening day of duck-hunting season. To make matters more harrowing, the pilots were civilians and therefore prohibited from carrying firearms, a disadvantage for which a few pilots paid the ultimate price when shot down over enemy territory. After the night orbit program was canceled on Christmas Day, 1968, Roger started flying copilot, delivering supplies to Hmong hill tribes in the mountains, on U.S. Air Force C-123 assault transports from which the military markings had been removed.

Aside from the usual rest and relaxation in Bangkok, the pilots lived lives of dangerous anonymity with few amenities. Whenever the CIA learned that American journalists had gotten wind of an Air America base's whereabouts, the pilots and crew would have an hour or two's notice to dismantle and evacuate. By the time the press showed up, all they'd find were a few huts and some chickens. As "civilians," many pilots did multi-year tours of duty. Two hundred and forty-three pilots lost their lives flying for Air America during the Vietnam War (one hundred during the last three years of it)—and for many years only their families and friends knew how they really died.

Roger quickly learned that it was not like the movies. There was no swelling music, no convenient cuts. He was holed up in the cockpit—hot and hungry and nursing a bursting bladder. The whole thing had the claustrophobic feel of going through an endless tunnel, away from yourself and everything you knew. After each successful mission, he felt like the one loaded chamber in a game of Russian roulette had moved one click closer. Roger developed a nervous little gagging cough when he flew into combat situations. It was as if the tunnel of his throat was closing.

One day in 1969, while Roger was walking through a Laotian village to pursue another of his passions, photography, he saw an old Laotian man moving through his rice paddy on the back of his water buffalo. The man appeared ancient, with a wizened face beneath a conical straw hat, yet he might not have been older than forty. Studying him from the embankment through his zoom lens, Roger was struck by how trapped they were in their respective worlds. He wondered what the rice farmer's life was like, and who had it better: Roger, son of affluence and citizen of the strongest nation on earth, who couldn't say exactly why he was flying secret supply missions to Hmong tribesmen in Laos, or the man who knew, day after day after day, that his place was with his water buffalo?

As a boy, he had watched his father, a product of the Great Depression, worship at the altar of financial security along with so many men of that generation. To support his lifestyle—the two country clubs, the racehorses, the gambling habit—John Brooks eventually had to borrow freely from his car dealerships, never claiming the loans as salary. When the IRS caught up with him, he had to sell his house and businesses to raise money for back taxes. The family was forced to exchange the large Orinda, California, house for a Phoenix rental. He tried to win his former life back at the track, and when Roger's mother discovered—she had never really peeked at her husband's finances before—that they were down to their last $100, she took a secretarial job to help the family slowly fight its way back to solvency. But the taint of money, and the stain of its lack, colored Roger's adolescence. The IRS hounded John Brooks for so many years that he was eventually on a first-name basis with almost everyone in the Phoenix office. Observing this, Roger never acquired much of a taste for materialism.

THERE WERE ANY NUMBER of pursuits for which the trick of intelligent detachment was an advantage, but being a green pilot on secret missions in Laos was not one of them. Yet there he was, getting to know the locals, standing outside his own country, his mind filling with questions. Was he really better off? Was America? Who and what were the forces that had moved him across the world to dodge antiaircraft artillery fire in a shadowy war? Alone among his colleagues, all of them older

and military-trained, Roger felt that, in terms of who was helping the Laotian people more, he was on the wrong side. A large
slice of his generation was experiencing feelings of betrayal on
college campuses; Roger was experiencing them in the belly of
the military-industrial complex. Like everyone who feels the
first chill of looking through the shell of the observable world at
the dark machinery inside, Roger was disturbed. He waited for
the feeling to go away. And it did, but only to return, again and
again, in ever more intricate forms.

On leave back in the United States, he watched President
Johnson talk about the war on TV. The lies leapt out at him.
The president assured the nation that the U.S. military was
merely flying armed reconnaissance over Laos, with instructions to fire only if fired upon, when Roger knew firsthand that
they were bombing the hell out of the place. A hundred years
before, America had overpowered the civilizations that had
preceded it in the West, and now it was trying to overwhelm another part of the world. Roger was already well schooled in the
strange-bedfellows aspect of geopolitics. It didn't take a genius
to realize that our government was not simply supporting mon-
sters, but sometimes creating them as well.

By July 1969, he had had enough. He left Air America,
flirted with expatriation in Germany and Sweden, then returned to the States to become an airline pilot. For much of his
career as a commercial pilot, Roger was an airline-safety activist, obsessively defending and protecting the safety of passengers against any action by industry or government that
compromised it. In the 1980s, for example, as chairman of

Frontier Airlines' Air Safety Committee and chairman of the Air Line Pilots Association's Accident Survival Committee, Roger confronted the Federal Aviation Administration over a regulation that it had secretly approved to *eliminate* two emergency exits on several airplanes, including the 747. The new regulation, of course, would make it harder than before to evacuate the plane in an emergency. To read the transcript of Roger's comments at a 1986 international air-safety symposium in Seattle is to get the sense that Roger was something of a buffalo himself—gentle until his interests were threatened and much smarter than he looked.

"It is well known in the aviation industry," he said, addressing the heads of Aircraft Certification for the FAA and for Boeing, "that [the Air Line Pilots Association], in the strongest terms, protested the unwise, callous, and self-serving decision by some Boeing 747 series 100, 200, and 300 operators [airlines] to remove existing emergency exits from their aircraft and to order new aircraft without these exits. . . . It is interesting, even curious, that only one public defender of this action exists: the Federal Aviation Administration. We have yet to receive an explanation from the manufacturer as to why exit pair number three should be removed. We have yet to hear from an operator detailing the financial benefits of such a change. Surely, we don't have a modification that has no benefits but only exists because it's labeled 'legal.' "

Boeing's head of aircraft certification rose in response. "Those pairs of exits were removed because of the interest of our customers to have airplane configured in that arrangement, to operate in the 440-or-below seating density. . . ."

Roger had never suffered double-talk gladly. "I would be very curious to know what your customer requests were," he said, "and who wanted this, and for what reasons, and whether there's a cost benefit on it, or what kind of payback period, or how much money could be saved by incurring the expense of removing exits. . . . I really think that for us to understand this particular removal—I think that the public really deserves to know who is benefiting and why, and perhaps you'd like to introduce that here."

Roger then proceeded to criticize Boeing for conducting inadequate emergency-exit tests to justify their decision—tests that were not in full compliance with strict FAA regulations, but which were nonetheless used as the basis for extrapolating "applicable" results. "I think full-scale demonstrations were required at that time," Roger said. "And the Boeing Company in that test did not [comply]. . . . And that test became your baseline for analysis, or a 'give me' factor that I'm sure Jack Nicklaus would like to have when he plays golf. . . .

"Now, as an airline captain," he continued, "I'm required to take a check ride every six months. And in no instance have I ever passed a check ride by analysis, based upon my previous performance." At this point the audience laughed—at least that portion of it enjoying the methodical way in which Roger Brooks was taking Boeing's—and the FAA's—case apart. "And if I can't do that, then I don't think you should be able to do that, either.

"The customers wanted it," Roger concluded. "But I don't think the customers' customers want it. And I think that's the point here, that there is an economy involved in doing this.

That economy is not passed on to the airline customers. Their safety is being degraded at no benefit whatsoever to them. And I don't think that that is legitimate. I don't think that is an honorable philosophy to use in this industry."

Shortly after the symposium, for the first time in its history the FAA effectively rescinded a regulation. An FAA administrator wrote a letter to all of the airlines, informing them that, while removing the No. 3 pair of emergency exits over the wings on a Boeing 747 was legal, they didn't recommend doing it. Nobody did. Before long, the FAA created a rule stipulating that there had to be no more than sixty-six feet between emergency exits on a commercial airplane. That rule, thanks to Roger Brooks, is still in effect today and applies to all new aircraft.

Later, Roger became the litigation manager on behalf of Frontier Airlines pilots, and spent part of almost every day for eight years preparing suits against two major airlines, United and Continental. When the Air Line Pilots Association union leaders shrank from the legal fight, Roger pursued it himself, from court to court, with some of the appeals reaching the United States Supreme Court.

The smaller-minded often make the mistake of ascribing to people of integrity one of two qualities: a superior morality that enables them to resist the easy choice or, on the other hand, a kind of vanity that motivates them to do the right thing in order to feel morally superior. At least for Roger, something much simpler was at work. Roger felt the sort of resistance to irresponsibility that everyone would feel about crossing the yellow dividing line and driving into oncoming traffic. It was not open to discussion, but an imperative for self-survival.

Roger's character was the sum of a lot of decisions other people might not have made, and the decision to honor his commitment to Charlie was just one of them.

ten

"He did just fine," Dr. Callan came out and told them an hour later. "Your boy's just fine."

"That's fantastic," Veryl said, exhaling with relief.

"What's the diagnosis?" Roger asked.

"Acute trauma with some movement of the vertebrae, which we expected," he said. "But the vertebrae C2 and C3 are back pretty much in their basic position. That's to say that Charlie's spinal cord is intact, but when there's a trauma like this, there's acute shock from the force of the blow and it disrupts the neurons going back and forth. The messages aren't getting from the brain to the rest of the body. Sometimes the nerves die."

"But other times," Veryl said hopefully, "they heal."

Dr. Callan nodded. "That's right. Sometimes they heal. Only time will tell. We're going to keep him on plenty of steroids to keep the swelling down. Best thing that's happened so far is that Charlie got steroids right away after the accident. Otherwise, the prognosis would be worse. I'd like to get him some acupuncture to relieve the pain and get the blood flowing in the injured areas." Callan looked at them with quiet compassion. "You folks going to stick around for a few days?"

"Of course," Roger said.

"Good. That'll be the best medicine of all."

When the doctor had gone, Roger turned sadly to Veryl. "Even *with* a miracle, he won't be pasture-sound. Charlie won't be able to stand in a pasture or pen without falling down and hurting himself. It's not good enough. If that's all he's going to be, not even pasture-sound, I'll have a hard time forgiving myself. It's all my fault," Roger said. "What was I thinking, introducing him to those other buffalo?"

"Sweetie, it was both of us and we were only putting him back where we thought he belonged."

When they saw him in his stall, Charlie had tubes sticking out of him. Veryl and Roger stroked him as he emerged from the anesthesia.

"You made it," Roger whispered to him when one of Charlie's eyes slowly opened.

Roger and Veryl stayed in Fort Collins for five more days. Every morning, when they got to Charlie's stall, he'd perk up slightly at the sight of them and grunt. The veterinary team would raise him in his sling, which pulled him across the floor in its track, and the vet students would move his legs for him. Veryl and Roger whispered encouragement and rewarded him with carrots, but Charlie's efforts were so pathetic, his general diagnosis so grim, that the two of them worried that the team was only indulging their own desperate love for this buffalo that had suddenly entered their lives. What called for valiant efforts in the case of a human usually called for euthanasia in the case of an animal. They had to beat back their despair and pour all their energy into encouraging Charlie. If love and hope were capable of inspiring a badly injured animal to overcome the odds, this would prove it once and for all.

After a week, Charlie had become by far the most cared-for buffalo in the history of veterinary medicine. By now, everybody in the veterinary hospital knew him. "Chuck, you get better-looking every day," a veterinary student would say.

"Yo, Charles," another would say, aiming an index finger at him, "you da buffalo!"

"Hey, Charlie," from yet another, sticking his head into the stall, where Charlie was suspended in his sling, hooves just brushing the floor. "Hang in there. Get it? *Hang* in there?"

One morning, Roger and Veryl arrived to find that some of the students had left a present for Charlie at his stall door: a dozen bags of his favorite peeled baby carrots.

The agonizing days went by, with Charlie carried across the floor in his sling. Then, at last, one day his forelegs reached out uncertainly, almost blindly, to feel the floor beneath them. They found the floor and played with it, wondering whether to trust it—and themselves. After a few moments, and with the wild encouragement of the staff, Charlie's front legs and the floor came to a mutual agreement. He was standing! It was only on two legs, and even then not entirely on his own, but for an animal who perhaps had no business even being alive it was miracle enough.

He became more confident, but he remained in the sling. He was dragging his hind legs. His left one was too far under him, and the right hind one behaved as if it had a mind of its own, jerking outward in a wide arc as it came forward. But at least he was approximating walking.

By the fifth day, Charlie had made enough progress, just enough, to give Roger and Veryl the confidence to leave him in the hands of Dr. Callan and his crew. It had been ten days since they had jumped into the empty horse trailer to be at Charlie's side. They had other business to attend to, including three horses and four cats that had been left in the care of their assistant.

"We'll take good care of him," Dr. Callan said. "I think it's safe to say no buffalo's ever been in better hands."

"What do you think?" Veryl asked. "His chances."

"I can see how badly he wants to please the two of you. As soon as he can stand on his own, we'll send him home with you."

It was the second tearful good-bye in little more than a week. "I hate this," Veryl said as they began their long journey back to Santa Fe.

Four days later, Roger was in Las Vegas to play in an over-forty-eight men's soccer tournament, an experience that would have been a lot less painful if Roger wasn't closer to sixty-five than to forty-eight. As soon as the tournament was over, he showered, dressed, and limped onto a flight to Denver, where he rented a car and drove to Fort Collins. He knew from daily phone calls to Dr. Callan that Charlie was still unable to get to his feet, so he wasn't the least bit surprised to find Charlie lying quietly on his bed of straw, wearing his bright blue sling. When Charlie saw Roger come into the stall, he raised his head a few inches and grunted a greeting.

"Hi, Charlie," Roger said, reaching down to scratch the top of his nose. Then, without thinking, he ran his hand down Charlie's back and tickled him on the butt, just above the tail—at the same spot where mares nibble their foals to get them to stand up. And the most extraordinary thing happened.

Charlie jumped up. With the same effortlessness with which healthy buffalo can jump onto a ledge six feet high, Charlie was suddenly on his feet.

There was only, as Dr. Callan might say, one problem: Charlie had forgotten how to stand. Roger's touch had sent a "stand up" message to Charlie's brain that had, amazingly, made the journey back to his legs, but no "keep standing" message had accompanied it, so the only thing his legs were thinking was, "Now what?" Charlie's legs panicked. They started scrambling and running as fast as they could, not unlike the time on the tile floor just prior to his charge at the Japanese visitors. The cord that connected his sling to the track began flying back and forth as Charlie clattered across the floor, his pantaloons—the long hair on his forelegs—shimmying as he tried to get his legs under him.

"Charlie!" Roger shouted in a mixture of fear and delight.

Finally, after what seemed like an eternity to Roger, Charlie fell hard on his side and lay on the straw, breathing heavily. He wore the hurt, bewildered expression that Roger had seen so often on shamed or embarrassed animals.

"No, no, you did great. You're going to be okay," Roger said, kneeling to embrace his big head. "You're going to do it."

Roger and two veterinary students hoisted him up in his harness and slowly moved his legs forward in a walking motion. For the next two hours, Roger picked up Charlie's legs, two at a time, raised them off the floor and then brought the hooves down firmly. Over and over and over again.

When it was time for Roger to head back to New Mexico, this time it wasn't nearly as hard to go.

A week later, it was Veryl's turn to visit. When she came in the back door of the barn, looked in Charlie's stall, and saw it was empty, her stomach went into a free-fall. Surely, someone would have called her if . . . It was like coming to the hospital to visit an ailing friend, only to find the bed empty and the nurse preparing the room for the next patient. She looked around for a clue, for any sign.

Only then did she spot Dr. Callan at the far end of the barn. Smiling at her, he flicked his head in the direction of the next stall over.

Charlie was there. *Standing.*

Veryl ran to Charlie's side and sat down on a hay bale next to him. He grunted and took her fingers in his mouth and started sucking. With her other hand, she clutched his big head and kissed him above the eye. Charlie rubbed his head against her leg and she drew him closer.

When he tried to walk, though, he faltered. He took a step, but his left hind leg collapsed and he stumbled, then staggered backward like a bad drunk and hit the cinderblock wall, stumbling to his front knees. With great effort, Charlie clambered to his feet, lurched toward Veryl, and wrapped his body around her, laying his head against her waist. A buffalo couldn't come any closer to a hug.

"You rarely see an animal who wants to get better as bad as old Charlie does," Callan said, leaning against the stall's door.

"When?" Veryl said through her tears. "When can he come—"

"Not yet," he said. "But soon."

eleven

A few days later, Dr. Callan called to say that Charlie was ready to go home.

"He's doing great," he told Roger. "But, remember, he's a three. You're going to have to keep an eye on him."

On January 26, 2001, three weeks to the day after Charlie had arrived at the Colorado State University Veterinary School of Medicine, Roger and Veryl drove up to get him. It was her fifty-fourth birthday and Charlie's present was that he was waiting for them, standing in his stall. Tears sprang again to Veryl's eyes.

They backed up the horse trailer to the dock opposite Charlie's stall. Charlie recognized it immediately; he had always liked the trailer, had always liked to go places. He took one look and began walking unsteadily toward it. Once inside, Charlie lay down contentedly between the two rows of fresh hay bales Roger had used to keep him sternal and cushion the ride, then gave Roger an expectant look.

The drive home was the opposite, emotionally and geographically, of the one up from Montosa Buffalo Ranch three weeks earlier. Roger and Veryl felt as if all the exhaustion and anxiety had been packed up, crated, addressed to the past, and mailed off. When they got back to the house, Roger backed the trailer up to the barn and led Charlie carefully down the ramp. But as soon as his legs hit the red brick barn floor, he began to lose his balance. Although his forelegs were strong, the rear part of his body was twisted to the left, forcing his shaky left hind leg to cope with a disproportionate amount of body weight, while the right hind leg, the more visibly affected, jerked forward with every step. His legs crumpled and he fell on his side with a thud.

As Roger helped him up, he knew that their work was not over, but only just beginning. He made a path of wood shavings in the barn to give Charlie traction going in and out of his stall, which he lined with hay bales to break Charlie's falls. In other places he put down rubber mats. He would need to spend as much time as he could with Charlie; his job description for the near future could be summed up as "keeping a buffalo from falling."

The worst of it was seeing how much this hurt Charlie's pride. Roger didn't think he had ever seen an animal as depressed as Charlie was after he had fallen. It was difficult to witness helplessness in a creature so large. But accidents could not be prevented. The damage was mostly psychological. Now he was hesitant to look Roger or Veryl in the eye. His grunts had become low grumbles. Roger knew that if Charlie kept falling with any regularity, he would soon get discouraged and give up on walking altogether.

Humans have a hunger for hope. Wounded or diminished animals know when their time has come and slink or crawl off to meet their fate halfway. Most people tend to go in the other direction, frantically scanning the landscape for the faintest message of salvation. Despite the very guarded prognosis from Dr. Callan, Roger and Veryl had proceeded to build a house of hope that Charlie, they soon realized, might not be able to live in. There were dinners together when Roger and Veryl could barely speak to each other because the only things that could possibly come out of their mouths were things neither of them wanted to hear. They were so depressed by Charlie's lack of progress that sometimes they forgot to be grateful that he was alive at all.

For the first time since Charlie's first few days at CSU, Roger began thinking the unthinkable—that maybe Charlie wouldn't make it back, maybe he would never even be pasture-sound. If Charlie couldn't stand without falling when he weighed five hundred pounds, what would happen when he grew to one thousand, then two thousand pounds? Charlie was gaining a pound or two a day. Could his legs support his weight as he got older and bigger? If not, he would become a complete danger to himself and anyone around him.

Roger sat on a hay bale in Charlie's stall one moonlit night, pondering life's contingencies, while Charlie lay quietly in the darkness, his big head resting against Roger's leg, his indigo shadow spilling across the barn floor. If Veryl hadn't been sent a *Texas Highways* magazine feature about her ancestor Charles Goodnight, she wouldn't have needed a buffalo calf in the first place. If Charlie's mother hadn't had to make the correct evolutionary choice between her herd and her calf, he never would have come into their lives. If he'd come into their lives, but they'd owned other buffalo, they might have been able to keep him. If Roger had spent more time acclimating Charlie to his new life at the Montosa Buffalo Ranch, easing him into the new situation, Charlie might not have run into the fence, and he might now be living with a herd. If, if, if. Life was a few acres of experience enclosed by a fence of ifs.

Not much more than a hundred years ago, buffalo had been slaughtered by the millions to make room for settlers and cattle and progress and fences—and yet here was a single buffalo, Roger mused, unlike any other. How strange that so much of life took the form of teeming, meaningless masses, yet its highest expression was what happened between just two beings, even a man and his hobbled buffalo.

Over the next few weeks, Charlie became a little more stable and recovered some of his pride. He and Roger started taking walks again, short ones. It wasn't like the old days. Charlie walked crookedly, his hindquarters twisted to the left. He still hoisted his hind right leg forward in an arc. He was slow going up and down the small rises and falls of the hills near the house. Roger made sure he was always on Charlie's left, the direction in which he almost always fell. As soon as Roger saw Charlie start to lose his balance he'd lean his hip hard against him with all his strength; it was often enough to stabilize Charlie's five hundred pounds. But sometimes it all happened too quickly, Charlie would take a spill, and Roger would wait patiently for him to get slowly to his feet. To protect Charlie's feelings, he made a conscious effort not even to look at him. He would pretend it hadn't happened at all, except that when Charlie got up Roger couldn't resist the urge to reward his courage in one of the languages Charlie understood best—Carrot.

For weeks, it was touch and go with Charlie, some days better than others. Even on the better days, though, Charlie had trouble changing directions or turning around. He'd be walking in five directions at once. Then he was going only in four directions, then three, then two. There wasn't any one particular day when Charlie improved dramatically. It was like watching a lot of things—a flower unfolding, winter turning to spring, or a child growing up.

Then, like suddenly seeing your daughter in her eighth-grade graduation gown and high heels, there came one moment—a late afternoon when he watched Charlie trotting, however uncertainly, toward him in the corral—when Roger knew that everything had changed. He realized that it had been quite a while since he had last thought that Charlie might not make it. He and Charlie had graduated from uncertainty. Roger ran up to the house, tore Veryl away from her sculpting, and took her down to the pen, where they stood hand in hand in the thick light of the setting sun and watched Charlie lower his head and go to town with his sparring partner, the now badly beaten fifty-five-gallon plastic drum.

The next day Roger picked up the phone to tell Dr. Callan about Charlie's progress.

"His butt's a little twisted to the left and he doesn't like to put much weight on his right hind leg," Roger said, "but he's pasture-sound and then some."

"Great news. I have to hand it to you."

"He couldn't have done it without you, Doc. And everyone else up there. I'm really thankful."

"There was nothing special about the medical care. Just the buffalo."

"We told you he wasn't your average bison. You know, he's turning one year old in a month. Rob, what's a buffalo's life expectancy?"

"In the wild? Fifteen, twenty years. Their teeth wear out from foraging. Although I've read of buffalo who got so old their horns just decayed and fell off. In captivity, they can generally go thirty years, maybe more. Charlie could live that long."

Roger laughed. "Like a son who never leaves home."

THE NEXT DAY Roger was on the phone with his lawyer.

"You want to *what?*"

"I want to change my will to provide for the buffalo."

"That's what I thought you said."

"I want to name a trustee for Charlie when Veryl and I are both gone and make sure there's plenty of money for his care and feeding."

"You're talking about a buffalo."

"He's going to outlive us. You've got to come over and see him."

"If I want to see a buffalo, I'll look at a nickel."

"They haven't made buffalo nickels since the nineteen-thirties."

"So I'll go on eBay and look at one."

"You'd rather look at a nickel on your computer than come over and say hello to the most extraordinary buffalo ever?" Roger said. "That's very insulting to Charlie."

"Insulting? Roger, it's bad enough you're putting a buffalo in your will. Don't tell me he's got feelings too."

"More than your average lawyer," Roger said, laughing, happier than he'd been in a long time.

twelve

The fact that Charlie was out of danger and arrangements were under way to provide for his future care didn't make Veryl and Roger's job easier. The sculpture of Charlie that Veryl was now working on—"Tomorrow's Leader," she would call it—captured the paradoxes of a yearling bull bison. In the sculpture, Charlie is caught between calfhood and adulthood. His legs, a little too big for his body, seem to jut out in too many different directions. But his beard and pantaloons are coming in. His horns are now about six inches long, long enough to keep any remotely intelligent human at a comfortable distance. He has a modest but unmistakable hump. Although there is a balance to his physique, the weight fairly equally distributed front and back, all of the eventual mass and power of his head, hump, and shoulders is now implicit in this intermediate form. Veryl has given Charlie an anxious expression. Something unfamiliar, possibly threatening, has caught his eye. His tail is standing up, a sign of alertness, if not belligerence. Perhaps he has spotted a wolf at the edge of the forest and is sizing him up, or maybe he's looking at a full-grown bull bison and wondering, with all the insecurity of adolescence, how he will ever grow into *that*.

In a brochure for a show featuring "Tomorrow's Leader," Veryl would include a quote from the nineteenth-century naturalist William Hornaday on the subject of one-year-old bull bisons: "Like a seventeen-year-old boy, the young bull shows his youth in so many ways it is always conspicuous, and his countenance is suggestive of a half-bearded youth."

Roger and Veryl now developed fresh anxieties about how to manage him. Like the parents of an adolescent, they fretted over the right formula of freedom, discipline, and benign neglect. They lost sleep over it. It wasn't as if you could call 1-800-BUFFALO and ask a customer representative what an unusually tame teenage bull buffalo living alone needed if he was to feel really good about himself.

In particular, they worried that he might be lonely. The older dogs, Luke and Mickey, were no longer interested in playing with him. Especially Mickey, on whose favorite Frisbee Charlie had been inadvertently standing one day; Mickey's desperate, incessant barking had finally lured Roger from the house to liberate the toy. The hair on Charlie's forehead was growing in thickly. In time, it would be four inches thick, enough to absorb the shock of a frontal assault from a rival he would never have. In time, Charlie would have ten times as much hair per square inch as a cow. With his horns and beard coming in and his pantaloons making him look like he was wearing baggy clamdiggers on his forelegs, Charlie was no longer the playful calf the dogs once knew. To them, it must have seemed as if that animal had been traded for a beast who wanted nothing to do with them. The two newest additions to the Brooks-Goodnight household, a Rottweiler named Flag and her mixed-breed daughter, Annie, were just plain confused at first. Flag, however, turned out to be a highly maternal and solicitous animal, and soon she was accompanying Roger and Charlie on their walks.

Since it was buffalo that scared him off at Montosa, Roger and Veryl considered goats and burros as potential playmates. To test Charlie's sociability, however, they settled finally on a young Longhorn steer offered on loan by some friends of theirs. Roger and Veryl named him T-Bone—a name designed to inhibit any potential emotional attachment—and one bright blue afternoon they threw him into the arena with Charlie and watched while the two animals got to know each other. Or, more precisely, didn't. If Charlie were a five-year-old boy instead of a one-year-old buffalo, his kindergarten teacher would no doubt write in his progress report: "Doesn't play well with others." The report for T-Bone would have been even less flattering, and included the phrase, "schoolyard bully."

At first, the two animals ignored each other, so Roger and

Veryl left them alone. But after a few days Veryl heard such a ruckus from her studio that she ran out to the pen to find T-Bone mercilessly chasing Charlie around. She picked up a tree limb, jumped in the arena, got right between them, and started waving it around at the steer. Undeterred, T-Bone took off after Charlie again, so Veryl wound up and heaved the limb at him, striking the steer's shoulder. Then she drove him into the adjacent enclosure.

"It's not working all that well," Roger reported to T-Bone's owners that evening.

"We forgot to tell you he's got some Coriente in him."

Roger was shocked. Coriente was a rather hot-blooded Mexican breed of cattle—not exactly the assortment of genes you'd choose in a prospective playmate for an impaired buffalo. T-Bone stayed in his own enclosure for another week or so—giving Roger, as well as Charlie, some angry looks—before Roger had time to drive him across New Mexico back to his home.

Roger concluded over dinner one night that maybe Charlie wasn't so lonely after all.

"Sweetie," Veryl said, "*we're* his herd."

Not only was Charlie not especially lonely, but he was becoming more independent. Charlie didn't greet Roger quite so often with a grunt. Inside every young male buffalo is a loner waiting to emerge. In the wild, bulls keep mostly to themselves except during rutting season, when they rejoin society to escort, or "tend," the females of their choice in preparation for mating. They live apart from the herd, alone or with a like-minded buddy or two, the bison equivalent of two octogenarians on a boardwalk bench. For the first time, Roger had a glimpse of Charlie's solitary, dignified future.

For the time being, though, there was nothing particularly dignified about the way Charlie expressed his independence and territoriality. Keeping him in the backyard was no longer an option, given his penchant for trampling small trees or picking a fight with the lawn furniture. Charlie was now confined to the barn and fenced arena—at least in theory. Late one night, Roger was awakened by a noise coming from the carport and went to the window. In the darkness, all he could make out was the silhouette of a massive hump gliding ominously, like the shark's fin in *Jaws,* between Roger's Saab and his cherished 1958 Studebaker Silver Hawk.

The thought of Charlie absentmindedly dragging a horn tip across the paint job was too much, so Roger began taking extra care that the corral gate was secured with slide bolts against Charlie's growing restlessness and ingenuity. But to err is human, and one day Roger forgot to fasten the gate. This time it was a truck that paid the price. Roger and Veryl had hired some men to come over and drill a new well. One of them, Jimmy, smelled of sheep since he and his father owned a herd of them, and the odor was more offensive to Charlie than the workers' invasion of his territory. Charlie did not want to be around the smell of other big animals any more than he wanted to be around the animals themselves, so he ambled up to the front of the property near the road, where the drillers had parked a brand new pickup truck, and began pawing the ground and snorting and bellowing.

The phone rang in Roger's office near the front door, and he picked it up to hear Jimmy's co-worker on his cell phone saying that Jimmy was now standing on top of his truck, which a buffalo was proceeding to attack. Roger was out of the house in a flash, followed closely by Veryl, but by the time they had sprinted up to the top of the driveway, the damage had been done. Charlie had head-butted a big dent in the door of the pickup while Jimmy surveyed the scene from the truck's roof.

As humiliating as it must have been for a cowboy to be "treed" on top of his own truck by the world's tamest buffalo, it had to be even more galling to be standing on top of your own truck with a buffalo snorting at you from below while a middle-aged couple hand-fed him baby carrots and then threw a lasso around his horns and led him away like a rambunctious family dog.

Still, and with some regularity, when Charlie was not in a mischievous mood, Roger could now get him to come just by calling, and could get him to go in a certain direction just by pointing. This degree of influence may be no great accomplishment with a dog, but it's a rare cat who'll stand for it, and you had to see it to believe it in the case of a buffalo. It was no accident. Roger had long ago achieved a similar level of intimacy with his now twenty-two-year-old horse Kepler, and he'd done it through trust—by never asking the horse to do something when Roger was in the saddle that Roger hadn't already taught him to do on his own. Roger never had to halter Kepler until they were outside the pasture gate. He could get him to follow just by touching his cheek. Kepler was so attuned to Roger, and

Roger only, that he was never distracted by other horses. Charlie was the same way. On a good day, when he and Roger were together, nothing else seemed to matter.

Roger liked to think about the next step in relationships. He liked to think about it the way other men daydream about playing the Old Course at St. Andrews or skiing Copper Bowl in eighteen inches of new powder. He liked to think about building blocks of trust, the architecture of intimacy. He liked to think about setting the stage for the next stage. As a result, he had never given Charlie a reason to dislike him. Of course, a buffalo was not a horse. Horses had been bred to do man's bidding; as far as buffalo were concerned, man hardly even existed. They had never learned to fear man or, sadly, his bullets. Buffalo belonged to themselves, so the trust that Charlie developed in Roger had no measure of fear in it. It was Roger whose trust in Charlie had to be constantly balanced by a legitimate concern for his own safety.

Exercising Charlie in his pen was fraught with fresh dangers. For instance, Charlie had a new game called "Let's Pretend I'm Charging You." The problem with the game was that, from the human participant's point of view, until the very last moment there was really no difference between a buffalo *pretending* to charge you and a buffalo who is *actually* charging you. Had Roger been prone to forgetting, which he was not, that despite all Charlie's advantages in life and the refinements of his character he remained, instinctually, a wild animal, these were the moments when he would have been reminded of that fact.

Roger was careful to teach Charlie how to transition from rough play with one of his "toys" to affectionate play with him. For the most part, Charlie understood that a plastic drum was one thing and Roger's body another. The line, though, wasn't always precise. On a couple of occasions, when they were playing together in the arena—watching them was like watching a dad shadow-box or play-wrestle with his gargantuan ten-year-old son—Charlie used the side of a horn to parry Roger's arm. This was new. One thing buffalo always know is precisely where the tips of their horns are. They do not wield them thoughtlessly. So Roger understood this as a gentle warning that the boundaries had been moved, and the penalty for violating them would now be more severe. A nervous or displeased horse will get skittish and run. An unhappy buffalo is different; he'll simply lower his head, nose to the ground, and give you a good look at the lethal tips of his horns. Charlie wasn't above showing Roger his horns, and Roger wasn't above backing off from a fight he could never win.

Walks were becoming fewer and farther between because of Charlie's unpredictability. On one walk, Roger told him it was time to go back to the barn and pulled his lead in that direction. Charlie responded by "accidentally" catching his horn in the pocket of Roger's shorts. This was not one of the old buffalo wedgies of Charlie's childhood; this time, the bigger, stronger version of Charlie lifted Roger clean off the ground so that only the toe of one sneaker was still touching.

"That's not funny, Charlie," Roger yelled. "Put me down."

Charlie chewed his grass.

"What part of 'Put me down' don't you understand?"

It was as if the 230-pound man on Charlie's horn was of no more concern than a fly on his nose.

"Okay," Roger said, "I was kidding about the barn."

This made no impression on Charlie.

"Does the phrase 'No more carrots ever' mean anything to you?"

It did not.

"Charlie! After all I've done for you!"

For some reason this got a response, raising the possibility that a buffalo who understands "Let's go back to the barn" is a buffalo who understands "After all I've done for you"—which is to say, it raised the slim possibility that buffalo have the capacity for guilt. Charlie lowered Roger to the ground.

Roger rearranged his shorts, then spit on his hands and rubbed them together to clean off the dust from Charlie's woolly head. Because he was a man of his word, he let Charlie graze a while longer as the sun disappeared in a tie-dyed blaze of hot pink and blue over the Jemez Mountains to the west. Then, leading him along with carrots, Roger walked him back to the barn, thinking: a few weeks ago, I was worried that he wouldn't be able to stand up. Now he's using me as a human dumbbell.

"Charlie," he said when he'd gotten the buffalo back in his stall between Matt Dillon's and Kepler's stalls. "You know something? You're beginning to act a little like a spoiled brat. You don't like other buffalo. You don't like cows. I'm not even sure you like me anymore. These walks of ours can be a pain in the butt. I need to think of ways to keep you out of trouble."

As it happened, Charlie was about to get his first job offer. And, as hyperactive fate would have it, the offer came from some of Charles Goodnight's old friends, the Taos Pueblo Indians.

thirteen

Charles Goodnight's life spanned almost a century. He was born ten years before Texas became a state and died the year of the Great Crash. He came into an unlit world where the Plains Indians still ruled, and reciprocal brutality between them and the white settlers was a terrifying fact of life. He died in a world in which that conflict was a distant memory, reenacted in a new medium called "the talkies." He lived long enough to see some of the Indians he fought in battle become his colleagues and friends.

One of his great friendships was with the Comanche chief Quanah Parker, a man who straddled vastly different worlds himself. In a sense, the relationship's roots went back to 1836, the year Goodnight was born in southern Illinois. That year, in northern Texas, the Comanches staged a raid on the garrison of the extended Parker family, Baptists who were steeped in Manifest Destiny. Of all the tribes, the Comanches were most violently opposed to white settlement and the killing of the buffalo, and they would be the last Indians to surrender, forty years later, to reservation life. During the attack on the Parkers' fort, the Comanches massacred several of the men and took, among their captives, a nine-year-old girl named Cynthia Ann, who would be raised a Comanche, later to become one of the wives of Chief Peta Nocona.

Cut to 1860, twenty-four years after Cynthia Ann's abduction. During a particularly bloody period in the protracted war between the Comanches and the settlers, the Comanches carried out an attack heinous even by the standards of the time. A band of Comanches raided the cabin of a Mr. Sherman, who had moved his family to the grasslands at the edge of the plains, knowing nothing about Indians—a conclusion easily deduced from the fact that he didn't even own a gun. The Comanches arrived while the Sherman family was eating dinner, drove the family out, and, though sparing the lives of Mr. Sherman and his two children, raped the pregnant Mrs. Sherman, tied her down, shot a few arrows through her, scalped her, and left her to die, which she did the following day after giving birth to a stillborn baby.

Among those who vowed revenge was one of the Shermans'

neighbors, a young scout named Charles Goodnight, who had ridden bareback from Illinois to Texas at the age of nine and now knew the country better than most white men, and probably as well as some Comanches. Goodnight gathered some men to pursue the fleeing Comanches, but they failed to catch up. Two weeks later, Goodnight served as scout for a much larger expedition made up of numerous locals, forty-seven Texas Rangers, and twenty-three soldiers from nearby Camp Cooper. On the Indians' trail near the Pease River on the Texas panhandle, Goodnight found the Sherman family's Bible where the Indians had dropped it, no doubt by accident since the Indians were well aware of the bullet-stopping properties of books and frequently used them to stuff their shields. Under the leadership of Army Captain Lawrence Sullivan "Sul" Ross, the Rangers finally caught up to the Comanches and—as the first reports described it—killed most of the braves in a brief surprise attack during which they captured a squaw and her nursing infant. (Subsequent firsthand accounts of the Pease River Massacre exposed it for what it was—the slaughter of sixteen Comanche women and only one or two men. "That was not a battle at all," admitted a member of the expedition, "but just a killing of squaws.")

Back at their camp, the men discovered that, although her hands were dirty and dark from handling buffalo meat, the grieving squaw—she erroneously believed her husband had been killed during the massacre—had blue eyes and light hair. Some of the men remembered that twenty-four years earlier, the Comanches had carried off a white girl named Parker, and they wondered if this was she. Captain Ross returned to his permanent camp with the squaw and summoned the abducted girl's uncle, Colonel Isaac Parker, who lived not far away. The colonel knew that his late brother and his wife had called their daughter Cynthia Ann. When he asked the squaw her name through an interpreter, she replied, "Me Cincee Ann."

Cynthia Ann Parker, known by the Comanches as Preloch, cried throughout that first night, fearing for the lives of her two sons, Pee-Nah and Quanah, whom she believed to have been at the Indian camp at the time of the Rangers' attack. Assured that no boys had been killed—in fact, they had been hunting a few miles away—Cynthia Ann calmed down. But she never recovered. The State of Texas granted her a pension of $500 a year and some land, but produced neither, and she and her infant daughter Topsannah moved in unhappily with a succession of relatives: first her uncle, from whom she often tried to escape; then her younger brother Silas Parker Jr., one of two children who had escaped during the Parkers' fort massacre in 1836, whose wife punished Topsannah for calling her mother by her Comanche name; finally, to her sister's house, where Topsannah contracted influenza and pneumonia and died in 1863 at the age of five. Cynthia Ann longed to return to the Comanches, but her white family seems to have done everything they could to prevent it, consigning her to the fate of an alien among her original people. The grieving, endlessly displaced Cynthia Ann held on for another six years before essentially starving herself to death in 1870. She was buried in a cemetery near Poyner, Texas.

To the end, she believed that her two sons had been killed during the Pease River Massacre, but in 1870 they were, in fact, very much alive. Her firstborn, Quanah, now in his late twenties, was a skilled horseman and warrior and had become the leader of an elusive band of Quahada Comanches that was the scourge of settlers on the Staked Plains in western Texas and eastern New Mexico in the 1870s. His Comanches vowed never to "walk the white man's road" until defeated. His men fought the U.S. Army repeatedly in the battles at Adobe Walls, Blanco Canyon, and in the Red River War of 1874–75. He killed dozens—though, it is said, no women or children were among them, in part because he feared accidentally killing his own recaptured mother and sister. But by 1875, weakened by the military campaigns and the buffalo slaughter, Quanah Parker had no choice but to surrender at last and allow his men to be herded onto the reservation in Fort Sill, Oklahoma.

On the reservation, scarce buffalo meat was being replaced by government beef rations, but the supply was inadequate. In 1878, reservation officials finally allowed two bands of Comanches and one of Kiowas to set off on a buffalo hunt that took them down into the Palo Duro Canyon. But the buffalo, alas, were almost gone. The Indians started killing cattle belonging to a nearby ranch started two years before by John Adair and Charles Goodnight. And so it was that Charles Goodnight got his first good look at the fearsome Comanche war chief he had opposed for almost twenty years. Goodnight rode after the Comanches and caught up with Parker at sundown. After reminiscing a bit, if you could call it that, about the 1860 massacre at Pease River, Goodnight requested the chief's appearance at ranch headquarters for the purpose of making a treaty.

"He pointed out that it was late, his ponies worn, and his papooses tired," Goodnight told his biographer, J. Evetts Haley, "but agreed to report in the morning." The following day, Goodnight was confronted by Quanah Parker and several braves acting as inquisitors.

"'Don't you know this country is ours?' one asked," Goodnight recounted. "I answered that I had heard they claimed the country, but that the great Captain of Texas also claimed it, and was making me pay for it. . . . The controversy, I declared, was a matter between them and the State of Texas, and if they owned the land, I was quite willing to settle with them."

Goodnight's hide would have to have been awfully thick for him not to be moved by the situation: negotiating with the great but now muzzled warrior, the grown-up son of the doubly-abducted Cynthia Ann. Goodnight laid out his terms. "You keep order and behave yourself," he told the chief, "and I'll give you two beeves [steers] every other day until you find out where the buffaloes are." Quanah agreed and both men kept their word. (Goodnight liked to say he never knew an Indian who didn't.) The Indians remained on the ranch for three weeks, filling their stomachs, until they were ordered back to Fort Sill. Out of the long hostilities between them and now this imperfect peace grew a friendship that would last until Parker's death in 1911.

On the reservation, Parker reconciled himself to life among the palefaces. As if his mother's blood had taken command of him, the natural-born leader became a proponent of Indian assimilation, earning the respect of the reservation's federal Indian agents. He became Comanche chief-in-captivity, uniting the factions and convincing the last holdouts to give up. He did not forfeit his outward identity—he retained his native dress, his high position in the growing peyote religion (the hallucinogenic substitute, it is said, for the Indians' lost freedom), and his polygamy (ultimately six or seven wives and as many as twenty-four children)—but Parker was now his former enemies' most influential ally. He learned English, became a leading advocate of leasing reservation lands to cattlemen (from which he profited greatly), invested wisely in a railroad, and even sold his own cattle to the U.S. government to use as Indian rations. In addition to being an entrepreneur, he became a spokesman for educating the Indians, the war-bonneted leader of local parades, a friend of presidents, and probably the wealthiest Indian in America. In 1908, he even played himself in an obscure silent-movie Western, *A Bank Robbery.* He bridged not only two cultures, but two disparate eras, passing, as his biographer Bill Neeley has written, "within the span of a single lifetime from a Stone Age warrior to a statesman in the age of the Industrial Revolution."

Along the way, Charles Goodnight advised Quanah on raising cattle; was a guest in Parker's large house near Cache, Oklahoma; and was thought by some to have great influence over the chief. It was Goodnight to whom Parker finally turned in 1911 after unsuccessfully petitioning the U.S. government to make good on its fifty-year-old promise of a $500 pension and land for his mother. "Mr. Charlie," he wrote his old combatant, "I want you to help me with my mother's property. I want you to write your representative in Austin and tell him to look the matter up."

A month earlier, Parker had managed to obtain $800 from the government to finance the transport and reburial of his mother's body, which a son-in-law had finally found in Poyner, Texas, so she could be laid to rest at the Post Oak Mission Cemetery, near Parker's home. At her funeral there on December 4, 1910, Parker spoke in his broken English: "Forty years ago my mother died. She captured by Comanches, nine years old. Love Indian and wild life so well not want to go back to white folks. All same people anyway, God say. I love my mother. I like my white people. Got great heart, I want my people follow after white way, get educated, know work, make living when payments stop."

Less than three months later, Quanah Parker himself died of heart failure caused by rheumatism and joined her at the cemetery. The promised land and the pension money never materialized.

In 1957, the U.S. government ordered the removal of the bodies of Cynthia Ann and Quanah Parker, and those of seven hundred other Comanches buried at Post Oak, so the military could build a proving grounds for guided missiles. Cynthia Ann and Quanah Parker were reburied at Fort Sill, Oklahoma, in a military ceremony. In 1965, Topsannah's remains joined them.

GOODNIGHT'S INDIAN-FIGHTING past revisited him from time to time until his own death. Toward the end of his life, he was visited at home in Goodnight, Texas, by some Kiowas passing through. Among them was an elder who, as the visit wore on, described a fight between his band and some Texas Rangers fifty years before in Quitaque country. Goodnight had been involved in such a gun battle in the same place at about the same time. When the Kiowa recalled being shot at by a ranger with a six-shooter, Goodnight realized that the Kiowa was describing him. He remembered the incident clearly, but had always thought he had fatally wounded the Kiowa on his horse.

"Gotdamn!" Goodnight exclaimed. "I wished I had killed you at the time—I certainly thought I did—but I'm gotdamn glad I didn't now." Then he cooked a big dinner for the whole Kiowa party.

BUT HIS MOST meaningful friendship with an Indian began not in violence, but with a shared sense of irony. In the fall of 1866, on one of Charles Goodnight's trips delivering government-contracted cattle to Santa Fe, he decided to ride north ninety miles up the Rio Grande on horseback, along the black gash in the flatland known as the Taos Gorge, and see the Taos Pueblo Indians, about whom he had heard so much. He was thirty years old. There, on the plaza of the pueblo, one of the great scientific breeders of range cattle introduced himself to the Taos Pueblo chief and medicine man, Standing Deer.

The Taos Pueblo Indians had at that point lived in New Mexico's Taos Valley for more than seven hundred years and were the survivors of a long and difficult history. They had fought Spanish conquistadors and missionaries, other Indian tribes, and the white man and his cavalry. They had been terror-ized, "civilized," Christianized, shot, stabbed, burned alive, and hanged—but still they had prevailed. Standing Deer showed Goodnight all around the village. The plaza was—still is—surrounded on three sides by clusters of adobe homes, pho-tos of which have become a staple of American grade-school so-cial studies textbooks. Today tourists pay $10 to walk around the plaza—where tribe members sell jewelry, art, fetishes, and pottery sparkling with mica—and the ruins of the Old San Geronimo Church. For another $5, they are free to take photos. The pueblos are not just for show; 150 of the 1,900 Taos Pueblo Indians live full-time in the pueblo, just as their ances-tors did, without electricity or plumbing, never marrying out-side the tribe.

Goodnight and Standing Deer talked in Spanish, their one common language, and the medicine man, who knew all the In-dian lore, told Goodnight about a huge snake that the Taos Pueblo Indians had once kept in the mission church, and to whom the Indians had once made human offerings.

Goodnight turned his head and fired a stream of tobacco juice onto the plaza. "Human sacrifices—now, was that really necessary?" he asked in Spanish.

"Si, señor," Standing Deer replied. "Muy necesario."

"If it was necessary then, why isn't it necessary now?"

Standing Deer thought for a moment. "Well, in the first place," he finally said, "there are no snakes big enough to eat anybody. In the second, there isn't anybody who wants to be eaten."

The two men stayed in touch, nineteenth-century-style. In

the late 1870s, when Standing Deer was hunting the increasingly scarce buffalo in the Palo Duro, Goodnight stopped where he was camping a couple of times, spending the night there on one occasion. Their next meeting was far more momentous. In the 1880s, when the Texas Panhandle was newly crisscrossed with barbed wire fences, the Taos Pueblo Indians' old chief and medicine man Standing Deer, who had once known the land intimately from his buffalo hunts, became disoriented after a trading trip to the Kiowa reservation in Oklahoma. The truth was that Indians were getting lost increasingly often, confused by an endless grid of barbed wire that had rearranged the landscape. They no longer knew their way around the land they loved. Because the Pueblo people believed they were literally born of the earth, they had lost not simply their bearings, but the sanctity of their origins.

Standing Deer and his men ended up in the town of Clarendon, which is now just down Route 287 from Goodnight, Texas, east of Amarillo, not far from the JA Ranch. Humbled, if not humiliated, the Indians asked for directions. Unfortunately, a handful of well-armed desperadoes who happened to be in town got it into their heads that the Taos Pueblo Indians were actually Comanche spies, and were ready to kill them. The language difficulties did not improve the chances for a peaceful resolution. The Taos Pueblo Indians spoke only Tiwa and Spanish, which they had learned from the conquistadors centuries before, but the outlaws spoke neither and the situation was deteriorating fast.

Standing Deer pleaded with the outlaws. His only leverage was his one connection in the area. *"Yo conozco un hombre se llama Buenas Noches,"* he told them. *"El tiene muchas vacas, muchos caballos, y muchas todas."* I know a man called Goodnight. He has many cows, many horses, and much of everything.

It was at this point, with the tension mounting between the outlaws and the Indians, that fate arranged a coincidence so extraordinary that it would elicit only groans of disdain at any cineplex. If it weren't for the testimony of Goodnight himself, a man of unassailable integrity, no one would believe it for a minute. Goodnight, whose ranch was nearby, happened to be in the town of Clarendon picking up some supplies. "There was a bunch of desperadoes (hard characters, three or four)," he would recall near the end of his life, "who seized this little bunch of Indians, claiming they were Comanche spies, and would certainly have killed them. . . . By sheer accident I happened to turn up at the Right Moment. Standing Deer was doing his best to make the white people understand he was Pueblo and peaceable. I came up just behind him just as he was trying to tell them in Spanish that he was a friend of mine. . . . I stepped around in front of him and I never saw a man any more relieved than he appeared to be."

Goodnight explained, with his usual quiet authority, that the men were not warriors, but peaceful Taos Pueblo Indians and friends of his. The desperadoes, probably as intimidated by the coincidence as they were by Goodnight himself, retreated, and the townspeople soon returned to their other business.

When the dust had settled, Goodnight, who could easily have been an Indian so acute was his own sense of direction, teased his old friend.

"Surely you know the way back to Taos," Goodnight said in Spanish. "Haven't you lived in this country all your life?"

"¡Sí, señor! ¡Sí! ¡Pero alambre! ¡Alambre!" But there's wire. "¡Alambre todas partes!" Wire everywhere.

For many years, the rancher kept the Taos Pueblo Indians supplied with buffalo hides and tallow from his own herd. It was, from the vantage point of the Indians' lost supremacy, a small gesture of goodwill from a representative of their conquerors, but even so it was the kind of gesture few white men made—and the Taos Pueblo Indians were not above gratitude for what it said about the survival of decency. In the 1920s, when Goodnight was well into his eighties and Standing Deer was long dead, Goodnight paid a last visit to Taos Pueblo with his biographer, J. Evetts Haley. In the group photographs of the visit, probably taken by Haley himself, Goodnight stands among the Taos Pueblo Indians—bow-legged, white-bearded, white-hatted, and nattily dressed. At one point during the visit, the door of a room opened and one of Standing Deer's daughters, herself quite old now, burst in, threw her arms around the old rancher, and began crying—partly in honor of her father's long friendship with Goodnight, partly in gratitude for Goodnight's steady supply of buffalo hides and tallow over the years.

He was so moved that on his return to the Goodnight Ranch in Goodnight, Texas, he told his wife the story.

"And what did you do?" Mary Ann asked.

"I cried too," he answered.

In 1926, after a sad decline into senility, Mary Ann Goodnight died. Toward the end, she seemed to find peace among the buffalo, making a habit of driving her buggy into the buffalo pastures. She once disappeared from the dinner table and was found standing in a crowd of buffalo in the corral across the road. One of the cowhands had to go out and bring her back, cradled in his arms. The animals she once nursed, as it were, now nursed her.

Goodnight had outlived his wife, all of his old friends, and his fortune—some of it lost in a Mexican silver mine, but much of it used to start a college for the children of local cowboys, an orphanage, and a bank. He had no children and he didn't see much use in taking it with him, although it turned out that he was far from through with life. A year after Mary Ann's death, a twenty-six-year-old orphan and telegrapher from Butte, Montana, named Corinne Goodnight had written him, curious about their shared name. The correspondence turned into a romance despite their sixty-five-year age difference and then into a May–late December marriage. She lightened his last years, and more; remarkably, she carried his child until she miscarried.

Like Mary Ann, in his dotage Goodnight was drawn to the buffalo as well; when he was moody, his favorite recreation was to have Corinne drive him out among them. In the spring of 1929, Goodnight's thoughts turned to the fate of his late friend Standing Deer's tribe and what they would do for buffalo once he was gone. The culinary virtues of buffalo fat were well known in the West, but buffalo tallow had become something of an obsession for Goodnight. A decade earlier, he had heavily promoted buffalo tallow's medicinal qualities as a remedy for rheumatism, and possibly for infant paralysis and tuberculosis.

He sent samples of it around the country, receiving one encouraging letter from a Los Angeles doctor who claimed to have used it on rectal and genital conditions with "great benefits." To the president of the American Bison Society, Goodnight had written unprophetically, "I believe it stands a fair chance to become the discovery of the age."

Whatever its medical uses, Goodnight didn't want Taos Pueblo to be without tallow for a traditional ceremony in which they burned the fat as an offering to the buffalo nation that it might feed the tribe in the coming year. So, as Goodnight's health failed, he made a gift he could scarcely afford, given his now modest circumstances: he sent nineteen of his buffalo to Taos Pueblo.

After they arrived two hundred miles away, Chief L. C. Lujan wrote him:

> *May 17, 1929*
>
> *My Dear Sir and Friend:*
>
> *Your welcome letter was received yesterday and we are always glad to hear from you. But we are sorry to learn that you have been sick and could not go up to Goodnight [Texas] where they were loading buffalos.*
>
> *My wife and I sincerely hope that you are well by now.*
>
> *Now I will tell you about the buffalos. They arrived here good and sound and [we] unloaded them inside of the fence erected for them last Saturday, May 11, 1929, and they seem to be very glad to get off the truck. Quite lots of people went to see them, but they did not get frighten with the people at all . . .*

"Kind hearted words are hidden somewhere, to impress upon you," another Taos Pueblo official wrote Goodnight two weeks later. "Without going any further with our conversation with you, we sincerely wish to thank you eternally for your kindness, and the valuable gifts. We take great pride of our buffaloes and we are holding a great appreciation for you, Mr. Goodnight . . ."

Six months later, on December 2, 1929, Charles Goodnight had his first heart attack in Arizona, where he spent his last winters. He was up within a week, eating a healthy serving of buffalo meat and dictating fourteen letters to Corinne, but he was struck by a second attack. Corinne, who had nursed him back to health once, hoped to do it again. His spirits rebounded. He railed against the cook, drank cup after cup of his beloved coffee in bed, and planned a Christmas son-of-a-bitch stew—a dish whose main ingredient was organ meats.

He didn't make it. Charles Goodnight died on December 12, 1929, at the age of ninety-three—not bad at all for someone with a voracious lifelong coffee and tobacco habit (he quit the latter at ninety-one, but it is said he once smoked fifty cigars during a single day's cattle drive) and a diet that had consisted almost entirely of meat.

On January 4, 1930, a few weeks after Goodnight's death, Antonio Mirabal of Taos Pueblo wrote to Haley, "I am personally sorry to hear the news of Col. Goodnight's death. As I see to myself that if Col. Goodnight didn't gave us the buffalos we would never see the buffalos in Taos Valley . . ."

Goodnight was buried next to Mary Ann in Goodnight, Texas, in a small family cemetery on a hill not far from the railroad tracks. It's a quarter of a mile from his house, still standing but neglected, and half a mile from the rim of the Palo Duro Canyon. Today, there's hardly anything left to the town of Goodnight, but the small cemetery is tidy, its grass mowed and the handful of cedars as shapely as topiary. On any given day, tied to the cyclone fence that surrounds the graves, you might see an embroidered woman's handkerchief for Mary Ann or a few fresh bandannas for her husband. They have not been forgotten.

But the fact that Charles Goodnight had made a gift of his buffalo had been long forgotten by virtually everybody, including the Taos Pueblo Indians themselves.

fourteen

Until the Christmas/Farewell-to-Charlie party that Roger and Veryl had thrown in December of 2000, the couple was not aware that Taos Pueblo even owned a buffalo herd that grazed on the fenced land just outside their ancient village an hour and a half away—let alone that it had been Charles Goodnight's gift. Dr. Marlo Goble, orthopedic surgeon/buffalo rancher par excellence, happened to mention it at the party, suggesting that they all drive up the next day to see it. Roger and Veryl, who had only recently found themselves in the buffalo-raising business and were developing a keen interest in the whole history of the animal, were amazed to know there was a herd so close by.

The day after the party, Roger, Veryl, and Marlo drove up to the reservation and met Richard Archuleta, a stocky, cheerful Taos Pueblo man in his forties with a long black ponytail. Archuleta was now in charge of the tribe's always thriving tourism trade, but until recently he had been the buffalo herd's manager. He walked the three visitors out to view the herd of roughly 120 head, most of them standing picturesquely in the snow, oblivious to the elements. It was a small herd, as bison herds go. Once in a while, Archuleta explained, a buffalo would be harvested and the meat given to the "traditional" Indians, but the Indians generally had little to do with them and the children only occasionally noticed them grazing in the distance.

Richard Archuleta knew a lot about the buffalo, but not where they had come from. "All I know about these bison," he told his visitors, "is that they came from some Texas rancher."

Roger and Veryl might have tried to look up the rancher's name in the Taos Pueblo records, but they wouldn't have found it there, thanks to the peculiar way the Taos Pueblo Indians kept track of things—or, rather, didn't. Each year, a tribal governor and a war chief, as well as their staffs, are appointed by the tribal council, which consists of some fifty male elders. Each year, on January 1, when the outgoing tribal governor and war chief leave office, they box up all their records and take them away. Some say that one effect of the nineteenth-century destruction of the Indians' culture was to leave them homeless, and one of the effects of homelessness was the feeling there was nothing left to pass on. In any case, the new administration took over each year with no record of what had happened before. Year after year this went on, the records of one year being removed in boxes to make room for the new records of the next, so that the past piled up until it was a big mound of stuff that no one recalled. It was hard enough to find out who said what at a council meeting last year, let alone learn where a bunch of bison came from a long time ago.

Veryl and Roger only learned the origins of the Taos Pueblo herd a few months after their visit. It was then the early spring of 2001, with Charlie on the mend and almost one year old. A documentary filmmaker working on a movie about Charles Goodnight came to Santa Fe to interview Veryl Goodnight. He happened to mention that his next stop was the Goodnight herd up at Taos Pueblo.

The *Goodnight* herd?

"Sure," the filmmaker said. "The herd was a gift from Goodnight just before he died. I don't remember the details, but they've got letters about it at the Haley Memorial Library in Midland, Texas."

There was something eerie about the revelation. Here they were, the parents of a handicapped buffalo who had come into their lives so Veryl could honor Charles Goodnight in her own chosen medium. Now it turned out that their house happened to be a hundred miles from a buffalo herd whose founding stock Goodnight had donated to Taos Pueblo. It was as if Charlie was opening a series of doors for them that they had no choice but to walk through.

Roger and Veryl called Richard Archuleta to tell him about Charles Goodnight's gift and invited him down to Santa Fe to see Veryl's files on Charles Goodnight and to meet Charlie. When Richard drove over a few days later, he parked in the driveway close to the barn and the arena and climbed out of his truck. Neither the buffalo nor Roger and Veryl were anywhere to be seen. He stood there, facing the house, wondering if perhaps he had come on the wrong day.

Roger and Veryl were actually looking out the window of the house, trying not to laugh as they watched Charlie emerge from the barn, limp up behind the unsuspecting Archuleta, and start sniffing the back of his pants.

The only time Richard—or, for that matter, most buffalo ranchers—handled buffalo was when vaccinating them in the chute or "dropping" them for butchering—or, as Richard liked to put it, "when you treat 'em and when you eat 'em." So, naturally, he jumped when he finally sensed the animal behind him, turned, and found himself staring at a bison head.

"Whoa," he said, staggering back a step. "Whoa there, buddy." Charlie made a low grunt of greeting while Richard backpedaled up the walk, keeping some distance between himself and Charlie, who followed in a trot, escorting him to the front door.

By the time Richard left that afternoon, he had gotten to know Charlie better and made him a job offer that Roger would not let him refuse: to be the most impressive show-and-tell item in grammar school history. Not long after Richard's visit, Roger, Veryl, and Veryl's fifteen-year-old nephew Adam Goodnight, who was visiting from Wheatland, Wyoming, loaded Charlie into the horse trailer and drove him up to the Taos Pueblo grade school. It was a blustery, overcast, late-March day, more winter than spring, when Charlie sashayed gingerly down the trailer ramp in a bright red halter, all seven hundred pounds of him, and gave several dozen Indian children their first meaningful experience with the animal that had once sustained much of their culture, and all of the Great Plains Indian culture. Charlie may not have been a buffalo to himself, but he certainly was to the schoolchildren, who had never been this close to one before.

Adam Goodnight helped herd the children into a semicircle in the yard of the one-story school. Roger, holding Charlie loosely by a rope lead just a few feet from the children, told them the story of Charles Goodnight and how he gave the Taos Pueblo Indians their herd and how Charlie got his name—and even how he got his limp. Then he asked if any of the children wanted to pet Charlie. Charlie was only a little taller than a third grader at this stage, but his horns had grown to about six inches and a few of the children thought better of Roger's invitation. However, a handful of kids inched forward in their purple sweatshirts and turquoise parkas to touch their first buffalo, just a quick poke or a pat. Charlie stood there patiently, as if he had been doing it his whole life.

A Taos Pueblo elder, his face furrowed with age, sidled up to Roger. "I remember the bison arriving when I was a little boy. They came in on a convoy of trucks."

"You remember?" Roger said. "You must have been a very little boy."

"I was, but it was a big, big event. It had been three generations since most of my people had seen a buffalo. Many people had tears in their eyes."

So the thread had not been completely broken. The gift had remained alive, if only in one man's memory, as though waiting for Charlie, Roger, and Veryl to breathe new life into it.

"Why don't the rest of your people know about Goodnight's gift?" Roger asked. "Why don't you tell them?"

The elder waved the question away. "The young people don't care," he said. "They don't need the buffalo. They've got Wal-Mart."

Not far away, Veryl was standing with her nephew Adam, who was still directing grammar-school traffic near Charlie, when one of the schoolteachers approached with her arm around a shy Taos Pueblo boy from the class, about seven or eight.

"This is Sonny," the teacher said to Adam. "He thinks you two might be related."

Since Adam Goodnight, with his blond hair and blue eyes, could not have looked more different from Sonny, Adam and Veryl at first thought it was a joke.

But the teacher was dead serious. "A long time ago, some of our people decided to call themselves Goodnight in honor of your ancestor," she said. "Sonny Goodnight here is the great-grandson of one of them."

"Cool," Adam Goodnight said, holding out his hand.

"Cool," Sonny Goodnight replied, shaking it.

And the two boys looked at each other across a chasm of history, connected only by the silent heritage of a name.

fifteen

Shortly before he died in 1929, Charles Goodnight tried to donate the remainder of his herd of 250 buffalo to the State of Texas in the hope they would be kept in a permanent bison preserve. But the state couldn't come up with the funding and, after Goodnight's death, the Goodnight Ranch in Goodnight, Texas, was sold to an insurance company, which turned out to be uninterested in raising buffalo. The neglected animals migrated from Goodnight's ranch on the rim back down to the floor of the Palo Duro Canyon, back to the JA Ranch. The Goodnights' own "adopted" son, Cleo Hubbard—the son of his longtime housekeeper Ella Patience—tried several times to bring them back, but the herd, demonstrating its signature disrespect for fragile fences and human preferences, kept returning to the canyon.

After a couple of years of this charade, the insurance company got tired of rebuilding fences and announced a buffalo hunt in the local newspaper, which meant that the progeny of the buffalo who had been spared from the Great Slaughter were now scheduled to be the object of a newly commissioned one. Only a huge public outcry prevented the hunt from taking place, and by the mid-1930s the herd had made its final escape down to the floor of the Palo Duro, where they lived as an historically significant nuisance on the 100,000 acres of the JA until 1997. That year, the Texas Parks and Wildlife District rounded them up and gave them a new permanent home in some fenced-in pastures at Caprock Canyons State Park on the eastern end of the Palo Duro Canyon, a hundred miles southeast of Amarillo.

Like several other ranchers, Goodnight had experimented pretty extensively over the years with the cattalo, and, as a result, much of America's surviving buffalo population has mixed cattle and buffalo DNA. In 1997, the state of Texas tested the herd and found that there were only thirty-six pure buffalo left, which they segregated into one of the very few herds of purebred wild buffalo left in North America. But thirty-six pure buffalo is a dangerously small number with which to insure a group's survival. Since some genes—adaptive genes—are present only in some buffaloes' DNA, it's a safe bet that the smaller the herd, the more likely it is that genes important for survival have been retired. A diminishing gene pool threatens the survival of a species by limiting adaptation. At the same time, unfavorable genes are magnified by inbreeding. With fewer than ten thousand wild buffalo living in North American parks and refuges, many in small groups, the threat could not be taken lightly.

Roger and Veryl learned of this predicament in the fall of 2001, when they traveled to Texas for an art show at the Texas Panhandle Plains Museum on the outskirts of Amarillo. They met Montie Goodin, the daughter of Charles and Mary Ann Goodnight's "adopted" son, Cleo Hubbard, and therefore as close to a granddaughter as the Goodnights had. Montie was a cherubic white-haired woman who lived with her husband Emery in a house, where she still lives, built by Charles Goodnight for her parents even closer to the edge of the Palo Duro Canyon, just down the road from Goodnight's own house. If you were lucky, Montie might just bake you Charles Goodnight's favorite pecan cake from the recipe handed down from her father. Montie, who had campaigned hard to get the Goodnight herd their new home in Caprock Canyon, helped run the Armstrong County Museum in nearby Claude, with its substantial Charles Goodnight exhibit, which includes a fine example of Goodnight's invention, the chuck wagon. Montie is a woman so immersed in her family history that she has written several monologues in the voice of Charles Goodnight. "What a woman," Goodnight says of Mary Ann in one of them. "I do believe her only regret was not having a child. 'Course she mothered everything that came by. When we first got to the Palo Duro, nobody around but me and the boys . . . a fellow came through and left us three chickens. She named every one of them. Made pets of them. We never did get to eat those chickens."

Montie Goodin introduced Roger and Veryl to her friend Danny Swepston, a Texas Parks and Wildlife District biologist and the man in charge of the descendants of Charles Goodnight's herd. Swepston lamented the fact that he couldn't find any genetic matches for the herd—pure buffalo that wouldn't adulterate the Goodnight herd with cattle genes.

By now, Roger and Veryl were getting used to the serendipity that had entered their lives with Charlie. "Well, what about the Taos Pueblo's herd?" Roger asked. "They came directly from Goodnight's herd."

"The Taos Pueblo Indians own some of Goodnight's bison?" Swepston said, surprised. "I mean, I've searched all of Goodnight's commercial records."

"Well, you wouldn't've found them there, because they were a gift Goodnight made the last year of his life."

Swepston wanted to know how many there were. Roger put the number at about a hundred and twenty.

"And you think they're pure?" Swepston asked.

"You'll have to draw some blood to be absolutely sure," Roger replied and told him about Richard Archuleta. "He doesn't think they've ever introduced any other buffalo, except for some pure Navajo bison from Fort Wingate."

And that's how it occurred to Roger that he might help

the Taos Pueblo Indians return the favor Goodnight had done for them, and in doing it help ensure the buffalo's survival as a genetically pure species. If Charlie could land a job as a buffalo ambassador to school kids, why couldn't Roger have a new job too, as an ambassador to the buffalo? By the time he and Veryl returned to New Mexico, Roger sensed the closing of a great circle.

Richard Archuleta set up the meeting, and several weeks later he took Roger and Veryl to see the war chief and five or six of his people in the conference room of their offices just inside the entrance to Taos Pueblo. Richard was excited, thinking there could be something powerful here—the recognition of a hundred-year-old gift. Roger and Veryl told the Indians their story. Charlie. Charles Goodnight. Goodnight's long friendship with Standing Deer. His kindness to the Taos Pueblo Indians. They'd brought photocopies of some of the letters. Nineteen buffalo, brought to Santa Fe by rail and trucked to Pueblo, so Goodnight's friends could have tallow for their ceremonies and food for the future. Here were photographs, visual proof, of Goodnight's friendship, pictures from the 1920s of the old man in a white hat posing with several Indians on the plaza—the very plaza just a hundred yards from where they were sitting. Why, some of the Taos Pueblo Indians were even named Goodnight. Roger and Richard told the war chief about the remnant of the Palo Duro herd, the spiritual and biological brothers and sisters of their own buffalo, hungry for new DNA. The three of them pitched the war chief on a donation to keep the bloodlines pure. Richard, who had served on the war chief's staff in 1994, casually threw out the suggestion: let's give them a few buffalo and then maybe they'll buy some from us later. Wouldn't it be wonderful, Roger added, to complete the circle?

In return, they got blank stares from the war chief and his men. Their suspicion was palpable. After what the white men had done to the Indians, they wanted a favor? After the rain of oppression that had fallen on their people for centuries? They were proud and independent. For centuries they had strictly enforced a policy forbidding marriage outside the tribe. Why wouldn't they view the mixing of their buffalo with another herd as another threat to the purity of their culture? Roger and Veryl left without any promises, or even any enthusiasm on the part of their hosts. They weren't even confident that the Taos Pueblo Indians had really been listening.

Still, the matter moved ahead a bit. A veterinarian was engaged to corral some of the Taos Pueblo bison and collect their blood. The samples were sent to Texas A&M for DNA testing, and the test proved that they were genetically the same as the Texas herd. But then a new war chief took office in January, the letters disappeared, the photos got lost or were taken home by somebody, and the whole matter vanished into the administrative black hole that opened up on Taos Pueblo every January 1.

There was nothing left to do about it then but contact the next administration and try all over again. But Roger's and Veryl's enthusiasm for the project was dimming. Charlie, a year and a half old now, began modeling for a new work of Veryl's, a study of impending adulthood she intended to call "Prairie

Contender." This time, of course, his modeling was haphazard; Veryl would drag her clay study out to the corral and hope to catch him in one position long enough to capture the lines of his developing hump or powerful profile.

Like *Of Mice and Men*'s Lenny, Charlie had no concept of his own strength. A hike was now a two-hour proposition requiring a second person to help control Charlie, and Veryl just didn't have the time. Roger had no choice but to discontinue long walks with him. For the time being they'd confine their work to the arena, and even there extreme vigilance was necessary. Being knocked down and stepped on was always within the realm of possibility. Moreover, Charlie's horns were now at Roger's kidney level. Marlo Goble recommended that Roger wear a protective bull-rider's vest, but he settled instead for keeping a cattle prod near the arena. Roger only had to use it once while working with him. In a last-ditch effort to make Charlie a somewhat safer companion, Roger cut holes in tennis balls and put them on the tips of Charlie's horns, but his dignity was insulted and he kept flinging them off. Friends and other visitors were strongly cautioned to keep a fence between them and the buffalo they had come to see.

In late fall of 2001, Charlie did manage to escape his arena again and cause a little trouble when a UPS delivery truck driver pulling into the driveway was perplexed to see a nearly grown buffalo approaching him. Veryl ran out of the house with a camera. So it was that shortly before Christmas, Roger and Veryl e-mailed their friends a Happy Holidays greeting whose subject line read: Santa's Little Helper. Below it was a photo of two of the largest brown objects in the world: one-and-a-half-year-old Charlie standing in profile in front of a UPS delivery truck, both of them facing in the same direction. The delighted UPS driver is leaning out the open truck door, reaching to pet Charlie, whose deadpan expression seems to be saying, "I don't know what it is, but they all want a piece of me."

sixteen

Yellowstone National Park, six hundred miles north of Santa Fe, represented one of the few efforts to save the buffalo by a country that had presided over their destruction and then, for years after, still didn't seem to care about them. Over the winter of 2001 and into the spring of 2002, it was getting harder and harder for Roger, Veryl, and a lot of other people to remain unaware of a situation there for which the word "irony" didn't quite seem sufficient. More than two hundred buffalo in America's last pure, wild, free-roaming herd—a herd to which Charles Goodnight had contributed three breeding bull bison in 1902—had been killed, not by hunters or poachers, but by employees of the Montana Department of Livestock. The clash in

and around Yellowstone between the buffalo and "civilization," between the ideology of wildlife conservation and the
mythology of the Old West, was yet another disturbing example of Faulkner's famous adage that "The past isn't dead; it isn't
even past." The immense political power of the cattle industry
was once again being brought to bear on the largest land mammal in North America, and the result was one of the bloodiest
years, and the bloodiest period, for the buffalo since the 1870s.

The Yellowstone herd had started as a handful of animals
who'd escaped the slaughter and taken refuge in what had, in
1872, become the country's first national park. Over the past
century, the herd had grown into a popular tourist attraction
that numbered somewhere around four thousand. Because of
severe winters and the herd's growing size, in late spring and
early winter some of Yellowstone's Lamar Valley buffalo migrated in single file across the park's invisible northern and
western borders on their way to lower-elevation public and private land in search of early grasses and better birthing grounds.
Before spring turned to summer, they returned to the park. On
their way out, however, they left Wyoming and crossed a few
miles of private Montana land, and that's where the trouble
began.

Inside the Park, the National Park Service was the agency in
charge of managing the buffalo, but after years of pressure from
Montana's livestock industry, the federal government had
handed over management of the buffalo, once they left Yellowstone, to Montana's Department of Livestock, an agency with
no other responsibilities for any other wild animals and a
strong prejudice against buffalo. The bias wasn't surprising,

given that the department's job was to "safeguard the health and food production capacity of the State's animals and poultry" and to "help minimize economic losses to livestock producers." The successful evolution of the cattle industry, after all, had depended on the elimination of the buffalo more than a century earlier.

Leaving the swashbuckling DOL agents in charge of buffalo who cross the invisible western border of Yellowstone in search of food was a little like letting a group of professional wrestlers teach a class of rambunctious schoolchildren: someone was going to get hurt, and it wasn't the grown-ups. Motivated by a trigger-happy combination of the need to control the local buffalo population, the fear of buffalo expansionism in general, and a largely hysterical fear that buffalo would transmit disease to nearby cattle, DOL agents killed 569 wayward bison during the winter of 1988–89, a dramatic increase over the occasional killing of previous years. In 1991–92, 271 more were slaughtered. In 1992–93, seventy-nine more. A quiet year followed. Then, between 1994 and 1997, 1,944 buffalo—more than half the buffalo population of Yellowstone in a given year—were killed, mostly by the Montana Department of Livestock, some of them in front of tourists.

The bad press that followed this surge of killing—shooting buffalo has been accurately compared to shooting a parked car—embarrassed the state of Montana, whose DOL agents then began to emphasize another tactic: hazing wandering buffalo back into the park by chasing them on horseback, snowmobiles, and all-terrain vehicles. They even used a helicopter flying illegally low, in flagrant violation of federal air regulations. The situation had more than faint echoes of hunting buffalo from the safety of a nineteenth-century train's parlor car. Other bison were hazed and herded into capture facilities just outside the park, from which many then proceeded to the slaughterhouse without testing for brucellosis, a disease that can cause cattle to abort, but only under circumstances so rare that transmission of it in the wild had not even been documented. In the loud chaos of these efforts, panicked buffalo were routinely injured, or aborted, or were separated from their newborns.

Montana mounted a public-relations campaign to soothe troubled brows, but stray buffalo had triggered an atavistic response in cattle people that could not easily be subdued. As an official with the Wyoming Department of Game and Fish told a reporter in 1997, "If the public gets used to the idea that bison, like elk and deer, should be free to roam on federal lands . . . then it may lead to a reduction in the amount of public-lands forage allotted to livestock. That's what the ranchers really fear." Jim Garry, a naturalist and author and an instructor at the Yellowstone Institute, expressed the prevailing fear another way: "Yellowstone bison would be happy to leave the park, colonize the whole Paradise Valley, turn right, and take over the plains." This is not paranoia, strictly speaking, thanks to regional planner Frank Popper and his geographer wife Deborah, who in 1987 shook the West up with their quite serious, though highly metaphorical, proposal for a "Buffalo Commons." The two academics, supported by U.S. Census Bureau and other difficult-to-refute statistics, documented that a quarter of the area of the ten Plains states was economically depressed, depopulating, and agriculturally exhausted—and that the best solution was to turn that land into an ecological reserve that, with the help of returning buffalo herds, would return the Plains to its former, natural pre-cattle glory. "What we never counted on," Frank Popper told the journalist and author Anne Matthews back in the early 1990s, "was the way the image of returning buffalo appears to touch on some primal apocalyptic terror."

By the late 1990s, the violence against the Yellowstone buffalo had created its own opposition—a nonprofit grassroots coalition of Native American and non-native environmentalists had been founded to stop the slaughter and harassment of Yellowstone's wild buffalo. The Buffalo Field Campaign was a grassroots organization that lived communally in a rented log lodge near the park on the shore of Lake Hebgen, which is situated in a little finger of southern Montana where that state, Wyoming, and Idaho meet. BFC volunteers staked out the park's boundaries from sunrise to sunset in winter and spring, steering and escorting buffalo—their "sacred brothers and sisters"—back into Yellowstone when they could and putting themselves between the buffalo and the agents when they couldn't. Patrolling in cars, on skis and snowshoes, they videotaped every DOL action they could, including their own occasional arrests. In addition, the Buffalo Field Campaign lobbied in Washington for legislation to protect the buffalo from being killed with taxpayers' money; to get buffalo the legal right, like any other wild animal, to traverse private land; and to get the buffalo listed, finally, as an endangered species.

By 2000, the conflict was national news. ABC's *Nightline*

called the conflict "the most ugly, bitter, and protracted fight in the West. It pits the federal government and a ragtag band of animal-rights activists on one side, the state of Montana and its powerful cattle industry on the other." As then–Yellowstone Superintendent Michael Finley said on the program, "Some poor bull bison stepped outside and crossed this imaginary line looking for a blade of grass, and then someone either shoots him or drives around on a snowmobile and says, 'We're just protecting the cattle industry.' That doesn't sell. That doesn't sell anywhere."

But it did sell in Montana, where killing Yellowstone buffalo who crossed the line was considered essential to protect the state's livestock industry not merely from largely theoretical competition for grazing land, but from brucellosis. Stamping out brucellosis had increasingly become Montana's rallying cry. Brucellosis, an infectious disease originally brought over from Europe—by cattle, ironically—can cause cows to abort their calves. In humans it goes by the name "undulant fever" (for its symptom of fluctuating fever) and was once a non-fatal risk of drinking unpasteurized milk, but there had been only a single reported human case in Montana since 1995—forty-six all told since 1957—and none resulting from bison contact. Montana wasn't worried about people, though; it was worried about buffalo. The bacteria is carried by bison, elk, and other wildlife in and around Yellowstone. Although Wyoming protected its cattle against brucellosis with a vaccine called RB51, which was about 75 percent effective, Montana had chosen not to, even though an actual outbreak of brucellosis would jeopardize its federal "brucellosis-free" status and prevent the state from exporting its cattle without brucellosis testing.

How real was the threat of brucellosis transmission from buffalo to cattle? After all, it was this threat that constituted the bulk of Montana's justification for hazing, capturing, testing, and killing Yellowstone's bison. The first clue to the actual severity of the threat was that the one hundred thousand elk in and around Yellowstone are also carriers, but Montana, which profited from elk hunting, was strangely uninterested in the threat posed by *them*. The scientific fact remained that cattle can contract brucellosis only by licking the infected fetus or placenta of a newborn buffalo calf—and in most cases must do it during the four or so hours that the bacteria survive outside a buffalo's body in warm weather, which is when buffalo give birth. The odds of this happening would seem to be remote—and indeed they are. There wasn't a *single recorded case* of brucellosis transmission from buffalo to cattle in the wild.

The most prestigious study of the problem, by the National Research Council, whose members are drawn from the National Academy of Sciences and the Institute of Medicine among others, had concluded in 1998 that "The risk of bison or elk transmitting brucellosis to cattle is small, but it is not zero." To conclude that "it is not zero" is to imply how close to that number the risk really is. None of the Council's recommendations for reaching a risk of "zero" mentioned hazing or shooting the Yellowstone buffalo. The U.S. Department of Agriculture considered the threat of transmission "unfounded." Even most ranchers acknowledged this. Even the Republican governor of

Montana, Marc Racicot, admitted as much on *Nightline* in 2000. "I don't believe there is a documented case," he said before adding, with dubious logic, "and that, again, is the result of extraordinarily strenuous efforts to make sure that we eliminate brucellosis."

The state's "strenuous efforts," however, did not prevent the tens of thousands of infected elk from roaming free in the vicinity of cattle—although the National Research Council had already recommended that "Any vaccination program for bison must be accompanied by a concomitant program for elk." Meanwhile, upwards of $2 million per year was being spent to harass and slaughter Yellowstone buffalo to protect a couple thousand cattle—cattle that in fact temporally shared no land with the buffalo, since migrating Yellowstone buffalo returned on their own to the park a month *before* Montana ranchers brought any of their cattle to the same public grazing lands. And yet buffalo were being killed who didn't even test positive for the disease. They were being slaughtered after testing positive with a test that was only 50 percent effective—that tested only for the presence of antibodies, not the disease itself. This meant either the animal had the disease or was resistant to it, a resistance it would have passed on to its offspring. Buffalo were being shot without even having been tested at all. Males were being killed even though, as the National Research Council concluded, bison with non-reproductive-tract infection—males, that is—"rarely, if ever" transmit the bacteria to cattle or to each other. Buffalo were sometimes shot within Yellowstone's borders. Buffalo were shot even though, just to the south, in Wyoming's Teton National Park, buffalo and cattle *shared the same grazing land* with no recorded incident of brucellosis transmission.

Obviously, Montana cattle ranchers would be happier if brucellosis were eradicated entirely, but just as obviously Montana was demonizing a single species. Not only was the threat of brucellosis essentially theoretical, but the Montana cattle industry that this modern-day scapegoating of the buffalo was designed to protect was itself a relatively minor cattle-industry player, accounting for 2.5 percent of U.S. beef production. In the process, it used more than $100 million in federal subsidies and needed more than seventy times the land base of a flatter, rainier cattle-producing state like Iowa or Florida.

And yet, when Chris Bury of *ABC News* asked Governor Racicot whether it was true that he spent more time on the Yellowstone buffalo issue than any other in the state, Racicot replied, "It is true."

As Don Barry, the assistant secretary of the interior, said in the same program, "My personal feeling is that it's time for Montana to move on. . . ."

"The most difficult aspect of the buffalo work is watching them die," wrote Dan Brister, the Buffalo Field Campaign's project director and the son of a Cape Cod fisherman, who joined the campaign in December 1997, shortly after it formed in response to the killing of 1,084 Yellowstone buffalo the previous winter. "I was riding down the trail at sunrise when I passed a group of snowmobilers. The guns on their backs were for the buffalo. I turned to follow them. Suddenly they made a sharp left and stopped; they had found the buffalo. I pulled my sled between the men and the buffalo. I knew that's what I'd do.

There was no soul-searching, none of that. It's why I'm here. The cops cuffed me and the DOL shot all six buffalo while I watched, helpless. That was the hardest, the darkest, most frustrating thing I have ever witnessed or been a part of."

THERE WAS NOW a fairly constant flow of friends, acquaintances, and strangers to the Brooks-Goodnight ranch on New Mexico State Road 592. A Girl Scout troop, the CEO and other top executives of Target Corporation, a famous Apache artist, and old pilot friends all trooped over to see Charlie. Roger showed him off like any parent does a talented child, although in this case the child's talent consisted principally of coming when called and of licking people to within an inch of their lives. Roger liked to pull out tufts of Charlie's coat so people could see for themselves how clean Charlie smelled. Roger and Veryl learned only after the fact about some of his admirers. An Austrian couple who owned a house a mile away came up to Roger at a social function in Santa Fe and said, "Oh my God, *you* have the bison!" It turned out he and his wife had become very friendly with Charlie on their walks, which took them right by his pasture area.

Roger and Veryl took Charlie on the road once in a while, where he made a splash grazing in his own enclosure at a local Indigenous Animal Weekend and then dispensing kisses during Spring Festival at Los Golindrinas.

Being the center of human attention suited Charlie well, since he had sworn off his own kind and was uneasy around animals in general—his old canine friends included. When Roger went to Charlie's stall, Mickey, Flag, and Luke would follow, crowding excitedly around the door, desperate to be acknowledged, but Charlie barely noticed. He preferred humans. He could discern people's good intentions. He would allow a string of strangers to line up at the corral fence to pet his nose and touch his forelock.

In his presence, many felt that they had crossed the gulf that divided them from the wild beast, from that dark, loamy, wordless realm where animals go about their ancient business. Charlie allowed them to experience that other world at such proximity that its otherness was no longer just a figure of speech. As Richard Attenborough once said about a close and potentially perilous encounter with two gorillas, "I felt as if I had somehow escaped the human condition." In Charlie's presence, it was possible to feel that you had just been let in on some secret, or been given a sneak peek at the cards, that some fear had been subtracted, some awe added. You had been cut down to size, yet made larger.

As Charlie turned two and grew bigger and healthier—he had hit the half-ton mark by early 2002—Roger had to watch him ever more closely. In the corral, Roger had recently noticed Charlie eyeing him and flicking his head back and forth, a form of rutting behavior, and had to beat a hasty retreat before Charlie could challenge him. Roger didn't have to win, but he couldn't afford to lose.

Several of Veryl's and Roger's friends urged them not to keep Charlie. One old friend of Roger's insisted it was a question of *when,* not *if,* Charlie was going to gore him. Some felt that Veryl—the kind of woman who'll stop to pet a strange dog, discover a tick in its ear, and remove it on the spot—was the vulnerable one. But Veryl felt that those who believed that Charlie would one day turn on Roger with a vengeance didn't know Roger and they didn't know Charlie. Veryl could remember only two times when Charlie had really lost his temper. One of them was the day he had smelled strange sheep on Jimmy's clothing and chased the well-driller up onto the roof of his truck. The other was when Roger and Veryl returned from a twelve-day trip and Roger made the uncharacteristic mistake of saying a cursory hello to Charlie before heading into the house to answer his e-mail. Within minutes, Charlie was tearing around the arena, digging and bellowing. An irate buffalo is not a pretty sight, and Roger, realizing now what he had done, rushed out to the arena armed only with Charlie's hairbrush.

"I'm sorry," Roger said over the fence, "I forgot to let you welcome me home, didn't I?"

Charlie took one look at him and began to calm down.

"You don't mind if I come in there and give you a good brushing, do you?"

Charlie grunted softly, and Roger climbed into the arena and brushed him for fifteen or twenty minutes until all was forgiven.

Still, Roger knew it wouldn't do any harm to learn more about training him. He and Veryl left Charlie and the other animals in the care of their trusted house-sitter and traveled to Scottsdale, Arizona, to see the premier buffalo trainer in America, Collin "T.C." Thorstenson. Thorstenson had started breaking animals—mostly bulls and ponies—as a boy on his family's South Dakota ranch. When he was nine, his father had purchased four buffalo, but T.C. quickly learned that buffalo were not tractable like cows or horses. Not until he was a young man did he have a chance to really work with an impressionable buffalo calf. Poachers attacked the family's herd, leaving behind a three-day-old orphaned bull calf who bonded with T.C. much as Charlie had with Roger and Veryl. T.C. named him Harvey and added the Wallbanger in honor of Harvey's sire, who had a reputation for trying to run through barn walls. By the time Harvey was four, T.C. considered him trained, and by the time he was seven, T.C. was showing Harvey off by riding him in rodeo roping events. But T.C. and his unusual 2,700-pound mount were soon kicked off the circuit by the other riders, whose horses were terrified. Not long after that, T.C. accepted a bet in Gillette, Wyoming, and proved that a buffalo could win a horse race, and the two of them embarked on a successful career of racing—and usually beating—quarter horses.

In 1990, T.C. moved his training facility—including Harvey and two protégés—from Wyoming to the warm weather of Arizona, where tragedy struck. Some oleander, which is extremely toxic to animals, got into a bale of alfalfa and Harvey, who had yet to live even a third of his life expectancy, was dead within a day. One of Harvey's offspring, a seven-year-old, took five months to die from the same cause. The deaths were devastating to Thorstenson, especially that of Harvey, who had been T.C.'s son in almost every sense.

By the time Roger and Veryl showed up in Scottsdale, T.C. had long recovered from the losses of his prized buffalo, his business, and his beloved father, who had been killed by a bison he had trained. T.C. had built Buffalo Express, the only business in the world specializing in the training of American Plains bison. His "performance buffalo" appear in movies, commercials, sporting events, special events, and rodeos. Veryl's first thought on getting out of the rental car and seeing the wiry, tough, lean Thorstenson was that he must be looking at the two of them and laughing inside. In fact, T.C. did spend the next hour and a half warning them that, if they persisted in "parenting" Charlie, they were going to get killed. Buffalo, T.C. reminded them, had proven to be famously hard to tame. In the wild, they were ferocious when threatened. By the time a buffalo calf was a few months old, it was already too late to overcome his natural aggression. In almost thirty years of training bison, T.C. had trained only four that he could completely trust in front of an unprotected audience. Then T.C. gave Roger and Veryl a private demonstration of his own long experience with buffalo. He lay under one of his buffalo, pulled himself up by the horns, jumped astride him, and cantered clockwise *and* counterclockwise. Then he gave Roger and Veryl a look that said, "Don't try this at home."

"ARE PEOPLE WRONG?" Roger asked Veryl after they returned to Santa Fe. "Or am I an idiot?" They were sitting on their patio by the sculpture garden.

"There's one thing I know about you," Veryl said. "You've almost always made the right decision."

"What makes me think this situation is different from what everyone else thinks it is?"

"Because it is. Because Charlie's different. Because nobody's ever done what you've done for a buffalo. Because Charlie knows it."

"Charlie knows how much I love him."

"Don't think I haven't noticed."

"You're jealous."

"If I came almost every time you called my name, you'd love me just as much."

"Let that be a lesson to you," Roger said.

"Maybe you should hand-feed me more carrots." Veryl knew that if she were not an animal lover herself, and didn't love Charlie, it wouldn't be so easy to joke about the triangle. As it was, she actually thought Roger had the harder job—he had to compete with their Jack Russell, who slept between them and growled hideously when they kissed.

"What a beautiful animal," Roger said, looking off toward the arena, where Charlie was standing, still as a painting. "You think all this would have happened if we had a human son?"

Veryl shook her head. "Even if you had a son, you'd still be doing this. And he'd be doing it with you."

As the third summer of Charlie's life came around, Roger and Veryl had gotten used to the idea of living permanently with a buffalo. They ordered an expensive new horse trailer with living quarters so Charlie could travel in comfort. They had their eye on a ranch in Durango, Colorado, to give Charlie a home where their buffalo, at last, could roam.

While Roger and Veryl were trying to save a single buffalo, they increasingly felt in the background the presence of the others, the ones in Yellowstone. It was hard to cultivate one's garden when the countryside was burning. One evening in late summer, Roger and Veryl watched some of the amateur videotape that the Buffalo Field Campaign had shot to document the hazing, capture, and slaughter of Yellowstone bison. In one scene, two agents in protective suits got ready to dispose of a dead newborn calf that the hazing had separated from its mother. The Buffalo Field Campaign cameraman shooting the scene questions an agent in the foreground: "Do you have anything to say about killing that baby?"

"Back up," the young agent tells him. "Keep backing up."

The cameraman persists: "Do you deny chasing this baby's mother while it was birthing it?" In the background, one of the agents picks up the dead calf by its hind legs and drops it into a large plastic bag.

Two years ago, the footage would have meant little or nothing to Roger. Now, of course, it couldn't have landed closer to home. It was as if he was viewing Charlie's tragic road not taken.

Roger stopped the tape and said, "Let's go to bed."

seventeen

It's hard to keep some things secret, especially something as big as a buffalo. By the time Charlie turned two, word had started to leak out that a sculptor and a retired airline pilot a few miles outside Santa Fe had a very friendly 1,300-pound pet. So it wasn't surprising that, on April 3, 2002, the *New Mexican,* a local newspaper, carried a short article titled "Only in Santa Fe: He's a Nice Pet Buffalo, But Watch the Tongue."

It was surprising, however, that a red-haired Santa Fe animal chiropractor named Sherry Gaber read it. She rarely read the local paper. She was normally too busy treating dogs, cats, birds, and a growing number of lame and hobbled horses. The fact that she just happened to pick up the newspaper that day was, in her mind, one of those examples of the working of some larger force, a force that had appeared now and then throughout her life.

Growing up in Skokie, Illinois, in the 1950s, Sherry had been one of those girls always trying to help sick birds and dogs. She came by her passion for healing honestly, since both her father and brother were chiropractors. Sherry would drag sick animals home to her father, who had no idea what to do with the parakeets, but tried his best to help the dogs. One dog she brought to him suffered from paralysis of the tongue, unable to eat or drink. When Sherry's father was through moving the animal's spine around to relieve the pressure on some of his nerves, Sherry put a bowl of water in front of the dog and he began lapping it up immediately.

Impressed that so little effort could make such a big difference, Sherry decided to become a veterinarian when she grew up. However, she quickly abandoned her ambition when she learned that it would require her to give animals injections and pills. Sherry had grown up in a medically avant garde family whose members had never been given a shot or taken a pill, and she had a strong aversion to both. She concluded that it made more sense to think about being a chiropractor for animals. But she was only in seventh grade, and one thing led to another, and she forgot about helping animals altogether. Instead, after high school she went off to Palmer College of Chiropractic in Davenport, Iowa, the most famous school of its kind, to become a healer of people like her father and brother before her.

Right before graduation, she broke up with her fiancé. She

jogged to a Davenport park and sat down by a lagoon to contemplate her future. There, a strange occurrence reminded her of her forsaken destiny. She looked over and saw a squirrel lying on the ground, apparently paralyzed, able to move only its head. Since the vast majority of people on the planet live their entire lives without seeing a paralyzed squirrel, or even one that's having trouble getting around, it seemed like a sign to Sherry. She wanted to help the squirrel, but she had no experience with animals, so she went off to get a friend for moral support and returned determined to do something. Gingerly, she approached the frightened animal and ran her hand up and down its spine. How strange to feel a squirrel! The first vertebra of the neck, called the atlas, was dislocated. With her finger, she guided it back into place.

But the squirrel didn't move. It lay motionless on the ground for fifteen minutes. Sherry looked disappointedly at it, then settled in with her friend by the lagoon and talked for a while. Fifteen minutes later and without any preliminaries, the squirrel shot to its feet and disappeared up a nearby tree, leaving Sherry far below, staring in utter amazement at what she seemed to have done after all.

Years later, Sherry would look back on this moment and be amused that she hadn't paid more attention to the sign. Of course, by then Sherry had learned what most adults know: that in hindsight the road is always littered with unread or poorly heeded signs. For Sherry, the squirrel had been like an easily ignored tap on the shoulder. She soon forgot about it and moved back to Chicago to start a practice helping people. For many years, she treated all kinds of physical problems until one day she began to feel troubled, as though something in her soul was out of alignment. She wasn't enjoying her work nearly as much as she used to and wondered if there was something else she might do with her life.

Around this time, out of the blue, some of her human patients began asking her to look at their ailing pets. More signs. They brought them in after hours—limping dogs, listless cats, petulant parrots. One night, Sherry bent over a sick cat a patient had brought in. As she always did before administering treatment, she muttered the silent prayer, "May the greatest good be done." As she prepared to go to work, the next sign hit Sherry right between the eyes. In the corner of the room Sherry saw a tall figure, a transparent silhouette that appeared to be made out of magenta fluorescent light, all head and neck and shoulders. She had never had a vision before, and she was frightened enough that she was glad to hear the voice of the cat's owner saying, "Do you think Herc will be all right?" Well, Sherry thought, at least I'm not dead. The cat's owner seemed completely unaware that they were sharing the room with a huge magenta woman. In her panic, Sherry was about to ask the woman if she could see the silhouette, but when she glanced back the silhouette was gone. Utterly and completely gone.

Sherry sold her practice and went to work as a volunteer, cleaning cages at a veterinary clinic in Chicago. She did that for ten months without being able to truly decide what to do next with her life. Apparently, it was going to take more than a paralyzed squirrel and a huge fluorescent figure to help her make up her mind.

It was going to take a dog with irritable bowel syndrome. The clinic secretary's dog was suffering from it and had already undergone a painful treatment that hadn't helped. The secretary was distraught. Sherry offered to help. She adjusted the dog's spine and the problem went away and never came back. Then the clinic's veterinarian himself came to Sherry and asked if she could work on his dog, who had been having epileptic seizures. The seizures stopped for a year, and shortly thereafter Sherry enrolled in the American Veterinarian Chiropractic Association's school.

With her degree, she opened an animal chiropractic practice on Chicago's North Side, working mostly on dogs, cats, and the occasional lame horse. But she was growing tired of Chicago winters and felt drawn to Santa Fe. In 1990, she and her new husband, a recently retired financial consultant, eloped to a seven-thousand-foot high valley in the Sangre de Cristo Mountains. Her card read: DR. SHERRY D. GABER, DOCTOR OF CHIROPRACTIC, CERTIFIED IN ANIMAL CHIROPRACTIC, FELINE–CANINE–EQUINE–AVIAN.

She and Steve had been in Santa Fe for a dozen years when she read the newspaper article describing Charlie's accident and miraculous recovery. The piece mentioned a lingering limp and other problems that Sherry could diagnose from a distance as symptoms of a displaced atlas. Sherry got Roger's phone number from the newspaper reporter and called.

"I just read that article about your buffalo," Sherry told Roger. "I'm a large-mammal chiropractor and I'd love to take a look at him."

Sherry braced herself for Roger's response. She was well

aware that a cold call from a stranger promising to correct your buffalo's posture was not an everyday occurrence. She didn't know that Roger Brooks's buffalo had already enjoyed the benefits of acupuncture at Colorado State University.

"Free initial consultation," she added.

"Well, I'm willing to try anything that might improve his health. Come on over."

Sherry drove the five miles from her house to theirs. As Roger recounted Charlie's case history to her, Sherry watched Charlie patrol his pen.

"See that leg?" Roger said, "He has trouble going uphill and down. And he refuses to go in a circle."

She could see how Charlie held his head tilted to one side and favored his right hind leg. She saw how hard and thin his muscles had become up and down his right side. She could see that his spine was out of alignment.

"I think I can help," she said. Those were the same words she had used fourteen years before with the owner of the dog with irritable bowel syndrome. But Sherry felt she needed to bone up on buffalo anatomy before going to work on Charlie, so Roger gave her the phone number of Dr. Rob Callan up in Colorado, who was glad to send Sherry pictures of a buffalo skeleton. Sherry studied the pictures at home and returned to see Charlie a few days later. This time, Sherry was a little bit nervous. She knew that a buffalo was likely to give her only one chance to adjust his spine.

Sherry climbed on a big Igloo cooler to give her some height and Roger called Charlie over to the fence.

"C'mon, Charlie, c'mon, son," Roger said. "Got a new friend to see you."

As Charlie turned and lumbered toward them, Sherry thought there was almost something silly about him with his shaggy beard and thick thatch of hair, somewhere between an Afro and a Beatles cut. If he were human and this were high school, she thought, he'd be the overweight but cute guy who gets A's in Chem and plays tuba in the band.

"I've got to warn you, Sherry," Roger said with a little laugh, "that he's going to want to smell your crotch, but don't worry. It'll keep him interested and quiet for a few minutes and—who knows?—you might even like it."

"I've been around big animals before," she assured him.

Right on cue, Charlie's head, larger than Sherry thought it was possible for a head to be, emerged magnificently through the fence. His nose found Sherry's crotch and he began to sniff avidly.

With no time to lose, Sherry bent forward at the waist, reached as far forward as she could, and plunged her hands into the heavy coat on the back of Charlie's neck. Within seconds, she found what she had suspected from reading the newspaper article.

"His atlas vertebra is displaced," Sherry said. "It's interfering with his lateral spinocerebellar tract."

"Come again?"

"The lateral spinocerebellar nerve tract is the nerve on the side of the spinal cord that enables the brain to be aware of the different parts of the body. If Charlie's brain can't perceive his right hind leg, it won't send motor impulses down there to move it. Hold on—I'm about to adjust it. First I like to say a little prayer."

Sherry closed her eyes and prayed quickly for the greatest good to be done, adding a special prayer that Charlie stop drooling on her jeans.

She pushed Charlie's atlas partway back into place. Charlie backpedaled a few steps, paused, then moved forward again, settling his nose again between Sherry's legs. "Good boy," she whispered, then said to Roger, "He knows I'm trying to help." Again she pushed on his vertebra and it gave a little more beneath the pressure of her fingers. Charlie stepped back again, grunted this time, and again he returned to the fence. This time, as she worked on him, he dropped his head, as if he was relaxing into it. Animals would settle like that, once you'd alleviated some of their discomfort.

"That's a good boy," Sherry said.

After each little adjustment, he backed up and returned, until Sherry had manipulated the wayward vertebra back into perfect alignment with the rest of his spine. This time, Charlie backed up but didn't come forward.

"It's all about their pain level," she said to Roger. "He knows I've done what I came to do. He can feel it. He already seems to be walking a little better."

It was true. And Roger wanted to say, "Sherry, where were you a year and a half ago?" If Sherry had come into Charlie's life soon after the accident, who knew how much further along he would be? For all that Colorado State University's School of

Veterinary Medicine had done, and it had been a lot, including acupuncture, no one had suggested chiropractic. If, if, if.

"Look at that, will you?" Sherry said. To prove his renewed vitality, Charlie had trotted to the far end of the arena and begun attacking his plastic drum. He gored it with a horn and threw it triumphantly into the air.

eighteen

Up in Yellowstone, there was no solution in sight. The Buffalo Field Campaign activists were dug in, denying the reality of the brucellosis threat entirely and rejecting the idea of vaccinating wild buffalo—for which a bison-specific vaccine didn't yet exist, anyway—in favor of simply vaccinating Montana cattle. The BFC called for the opening of federal lands outside the park to the buffalo. They sought to have the buffalo added to the list of endangered species. All in all, the group was charging hard against the entrenched interests and mythology of the American West. The Montana Department of Livestock and other state and federal agencies sought to reduce the risk of brucellosis to that elusive zero, and they were making the Yellowstone buffalo pay the price while they tried. It was a good old standoff, and more and more reporters and op-ed writers were taking notice. Meanwhile, over the winter of 2002–3, 246 more Yellowstone buffalo were shot or captured and sent to slaughter.

In Santa Fe, Charlie, now 1,800 pounds and still growing, "modeled" for Veryl's fourth sculpture of him, "Prairie Contender." Charlie's uncertainty at the age of one had been replaced by determination. His tail was still up, but instead of wearing an expression that mixed fear and wonder, Charlie held his head low, sniffing the air, perhaps getting a whiff of predator or of the estrogen-heavy odor of a rutting cow.

In the spring of 2003, President Bush invaded Iraq and Charlie turned three.

Charlie had not been for a hike with Roger for the last year, and his life had settled into a slower, safer status quo. He spent all his time in his stall or in the arena. Except when he was out of town, Roger spent an average of an hour a day with him— feeding and grooming him, mucking his stall, but most of all working with him to strengthen his legs. He used carrots to entice him into jogs around the arena. He helped Charlie work on his cantering. He made sure Charlie got in a good sparring match with his barrel. The important thing was to be there every day, to have continuity of contact; otherwise, Roger knew he would lose his relationship with Charlie, the one he had painstakingly created, one unlike any man-buffalo relationship in history. Roger never forgot for a minute that Charlie was and always would be a wild animal, from his first breath to his last, and that if their trust was broken, it could never be mended.

An hour a day with Charlie was a lot of time, considering how busy Roger was with Veryl's flourishing art business, his soccer games, his reading, keeping up with his old friends in the intelligence community, and running a rather complicated household that had its own payroll. Veryl complained that he never rode Kepler anymore, his horse for twenty-three years; that it wasn't fair to Kepler. Roger would say, "Well, you're right, honey, but I don't have any more extra time, and Charlie needs it more."

Although Charlie was still at times fussy about being touched on the head and horns, and although you wouldn't want to leave your worst enemy alone in the arena with Charlie, Roger began to notice a mellowing in the buffalo, and he decided in March that it was safe to lift the embargo on long walks in the foothills behind the house. Roger was suddenly looking forward to hiking with him, the way the parent of a nineteen-year-old son might be delighted at the thought of having a civil conversation with him now that he'd survived the teenage years and no longer believed he knew everything.

As Veryl videotaped the hike, Roger led Charlie over the crest of a foothill, where they stopped, their outlines crisp against the hard blue sky. Charlie's hump now came up to Roger's head. Suddenly, Charlie, perhaps himself overjoyed to be out and about again, started licking Roger's face. Roger mugged to Veryl and the camera: "If I'm not faithful to you, it won't be on purpose." Traversing a gently inclined hill, Charlie was surefooted, although his gait was still not normal.

"His legs aren't injured," he explained to friends who had accompanied them on the hike. "It's all in his neck. He was getting pressure on his spinal cord from his out-of-alignment vertebra. But, see, by doing this—the walk, and I jog with him and chase him around the arena—it's going to get his brain working his legs better and it will strengthen up his right hind leg, and once he can push off evenly, he'll improve dramatically."

The walk ended with Roger sitting on a lawn chair and stroking Charlie's head, which was bigger now than Roger's head and torso put together. Mellowed by the walk, Charlie was enjoying this bit of intimacy. Although his horns were mere inches from Roger's face, Roger was as relaxed as if he were petting one of their dogs, but he was thinking: a buffalo dropped into my life three years ago and it has never been the same.

IN 1983, Lewis Hyde, a thirty-eight-year-old poet, essayist, teacher, and sometime carpenter and electrician living in Watertown, Massachusetts, published a book he'd been laboring on for five years called *The Gift: Imagination and the Erotic Life of Property*. It is not an easy read, combining anthropology, economics, literary criticism, psychology, and social history. Its index includes entries for Maori hunting rituals, Harold Pinter, property rights in organ transplants, Ezra Pound's credit theories, and McDonald's.

Like the kind of gift the book is a study of—a "transformative" gift that has "the power to awaken a part of the soul"—the book has circulated in a community of thoughtful readers for more than two decades. *The Gift* is not your ordinary fare and neither are people's reactions to it. The reader reviews posted on Amazon.com are a good example. "Why isn't this a classic?" a reader from Calgary complains. "The first essay in this compilation of three is one of those pieces that can potentially change a person's life," writes another from Concord, Massachusetts. And a reader from Kentwood, Michigan, adds: "I would rank this book in the ten most important I have read. His study of gift-giving throughout history and with different cultures changed my entire view of how we give and receive gifts."

One of the *The Gift*'s fans was Charles Goodnight's great-grandnephew Andy Wilkinson, who had sung at the going-away party for Charlie. A poet friend of his had suggested he read the book at a point in Andy's life when he was grappling with the distinction between art and commerce, and not merely in an academic way. For five years, writing and performing had been his full-time occupation—the kind of occupation that can make a person keenly aware of the difference between art and commerce. In an upper-level seminar he taught as an assistant adjunct professor in the Honors College at Texas Tech in Lubbock, he began using the book to teach that creativity was a gift. Because a gift possessed worth—was not a commodity with mere monetary value—people should not expect compensation for its fruits, he taught. Gifts, as Lewis Hyde makes clear, operate in a different and vastly more spiritual economy than the usual goods and services. Andy Wilkinson figured that teaching a bit of Lewis Hyde's book might save artists and aspiring artists a lot of grief in their lives.

Charlie had many of the attributes of a gift, as described by Hyde. A gift cannot be bought or acquired through an act of will. A gift is never used up, no matter how much it's used. The giving of a gift establishes a personal relationship between the parties involved. The gift must always move—as illustrated in many folk tales in which the gift dies because one person tries to hold on to it. A gift's movement, when it circulates, is beyond the control of any person, and it moves toward the person who needs it most. Hyde also writes about how gifts—whether a cheap but cherished object passed around by sorority sisters, a Mozart symphony shared by millions, or the battered silver Stanley Cup that passes each year to the National Hockey League's championship team—create and maintain "institutions of positive reciprocity." Without these institutions, people become disconnected and, in Hyde's words, "are unable to enter gracefully into nature, unable to draw community out of the mass, and, finally, unable to receive, contribute toward, and pass along the collective treasures we refer to as culture and tradition."

Andy Wilkinson, who among other things was a student of the Plains Indians and of his own great-grand uncle Charles Goodnight, was a person who deeply understood that for the Indians the buffalo had been, for thousands of years, a gift—a gift of nature, of the Great Spirit, without which they could not survive. Indians in southern Canada thought the buffalo were a gift that came from under a lake in modern-day Saskatchewan.

Many Plains Indian tribes believed that buffalo came from a big underground cave in northwest Texas, and that each spring the Great Spirit arranged for an endless supply of buffalo to pour forth. In his 1877 book *The Plains of the Great West,* Colonel Richard Dodge—the same man who once said that every buffalo gone was an Indian gone—wrote of more than one Indian who claimed to have actually seen the animals streaming out of the cave.

The Indians did not think of themselves as bigger or smarter than the buffalo. They did not regard the buffalo as being in the least subject to their will. As the Lakota medicine man John Lame Deer has written about the buffalo, "They have the power and the wisdom. He is our brother. We have many legends of buffalo changing themselves into men. And the Indians are built like buffalo, too—big shoulders, narrow hips." This echoes a passage in Lewis Hyde's book, that ". . . we cannot receive the gift until we can meet it as an equal. We therefore submit ourselves to the labor of becoming like the gift."

These ideas—that we can learn from animals, that they are in many ways our equals and our superiors, that becoming more like an animal is something to strive for—are open to ridicule and often lost to us now in the "civilized" world. But, for the Indian, the buffalo was sacred. "That animal," Lame Deer writes, "was almost like a part of ourselves, part of our souls. . . . It was hard to say where the animal ended and the man began." To kill a buffalo, then, was no simple matter, as Lame Deer explains:

When we killed a buffalo, we knew what we were doing. We apologized to his spirit, tried to make him understand why we did it, honoring with a prayer the bones of those who gave their flesh to keep us alive, praying for their return, praying for the life of our brothers, the buffalo nation, as well as for our own people.

To the Indian the buffalo was a gift, but to the whites the buffalo, along with its hide, its tongue, and its bones, became a commodity. "That terrible arrogance of the white man," Lame Deer wrote, "making himself something more than God, more than nature." To understand this was to begin to appreciate that the Great Slaughter did not just eventually deprive the Indians of material self-sufficiency, but also violated the spiritual economy in which the buffalo was the currency.

In this light, it was possible to see Charlie as a gift sent by Charles and Mary Ann Goodnight and Standing Deer into the present. Of course, this isn't much different from saying that a new puppy has a way of bringing family members together, of increasing their humanity, of restoring some of life's mystery by pointing out a world of feelings and connectivity that exists apart from the human language that often weighs down every human transaction. Except that in Charlie's case, the family was much bigger, the message much larger, and the present stakes significant. If he *was* a gift, he had been sent so that Veryl could honor her ancestors and the memory of all buffalo, so that the Taos Pueblo adults and schoolchildren could be recon-

nected to the meaning of their buffalo. He had come to bring together two young Goodnights, Adam and Sonny, and honor the
white man who honored the Indians. It was as if this gentle,
wounded buffalo had been sent out among the people so that
they could see and touch and smell a world that had been left
behind. So that they might "enter gracefully into nature."

Charlie was like a piece of the past that must be dealt with
before you can move on.

nineteen

Before Roger could move on, he wanted to make one more attempt to persuade the Taos Pueblo Indians to return a few of their buffalo cows to the purebred descendants of Charles Goodnight's original herd, still living in Texas, and help diversify the gene pool. It had now been almost two years since his first visit to the war chief with Richard Archuleta and their unsuccessful attempt to broker a deal. Among the gifts that Charlie had given Roger were a heart-wrenching awareness of the great injustices done to the buffalo, and a commitment to help restore the animal to its proper place on the land and in the American imagination. In the summer of 2003, the time had come again to pay the Taos Pueblo officials a visit.

Once again, he asked Richard Archuleta to make the arrangements. In July, Roger drove north into Taos to meet Richard at a restaurant called Michael's for a cup of coffee and a piece of homemade pie before heading up to Taos Pueblo, just outside of town. When Roger walked into the cafe, Richard was in his usual buoyant mood. Roger was contemplative. The prospect of a meeting with the new war chief didn't thrill him. To call the previous war chief "unresponsive" would be an understatement.

A little before three in the afternoon, Richard ushered Roger into the nondescript tribal government office building on the fringes of the picturesque reservation. Although Richard had made an appointment, the receptionist told the two men that the war chief wasn't in, but would try to find him. Roger rolled his eyes. Richard showed Roger into the conference room at the end of the hall and then disappeared for a few minutes. Roger sat waiting in a chair while a stuffed buffalo bull's head glowered at him from the opposite wall. Roger waited. It was so frustrating. Yes, he was a white man asking them for a favor, but it was a favor to the buffalo, a favor to themselves, really. Closing the circle of Charles Goodnight's generosity by making a few buffalo available to the man's original herd made sense in every possible way. What was the problem?

The conference door opened and Richard showed in two casually dressed Taos Pueblo men in their forties. Neither of them was the war chief. Vernon Brown was the lieutenant war chief; Louis Zamora was an aide. Everyone shook hands, Richard Archuleta excused himself, and the three men sat down at the table, Roger across from Louis, who sat right under the buffalo head, while Vernon settled at the end of the long table.

Roger fought off a creeping feeling of futility and placed his large freckled hands flat on the Formica conference tabletop. "My wife is a sculptor," he began in the slightly mechanical voice of a salesman on his last call of the day. "We live in Tesuque just outside of Santa Fe. Her ancestors, Charles Goodnight and his wife, as you probably know, salvaged some buffalo calves in the 1870s, bottle-fed them, and started a herd that exists to this day in the Palo Duro Canyon. So my wife could make a sculpture in their honor, we got a bottle baby ourselves to model for her, and right now he's three years old and still lives with us.

"Right before Goodnight died, he gave your people some of his pure buffalo as a gift, because of his long friendship with Standing Deer, and because, after the Great Slaughter, it was hard to get hold of the buffalo tallow your people needed for their traditional ceremonies."

"We're familiar with the story," Vernon Brown interjected.

Well, that was something, Roger thought—maybe there'd been some kind of carryover from two years ago. "Now there's no official record of the transaction because Goodnight *gave* the buffalo, not sold them," he said. "But we have documentation, letters which we gave to Chief Romero two years ago, but which apparently no one can find."

"They're probably in a drawer somewhere in his house," Vernon said with a faint smile.

"Probably," Roger said with a rueful chuckle. "So the rest

of the herd lived wild in the Palo Duro, from Goodnight's death in 1929 until 1997, when the State of Texas rounded them up and gave them a fenced-in home in Caprock Canyons State Park. They blood-tested all of them and extracted any that had cattle genes, so they're left with thirty-six pure descendants of the Southern herd. But they need new pure blood. And that's where your herd here comes in. Your herd has already been tested at Texas A&M. Your bison are a match." Roger then quickly added, in case the meaning of it all hadn't come through: "Goodnight, who was a friend of the Taos Pueblo Indians for a long time, came to funerals here and gave your people the bison when he was no longer a rich man. Now we hope you'll commemorate his legacy, his herd, by coming full circle and making a few buffalo available to the State of Texas."

Louis Zamora, who could have posed for the buffalo nickel with his aquiline nose and black hair pulled back in a ponytail, asked, "Do you represent the State of Texas?"

"No, I don't represent anybody. I'm not officially connected, although I have spoken with Danny Swepston, the chief biologist for the state parks and wildlife district."

Vernon turned to Louis. "Louis, I think we better get with these people and sell some of our old cows to them. The ones who are six to ten years old, 'cause we can't use them when they die of old age." He turned now to Roger. "What would we get in return? Cows or bulls?"

Although he had been thinking more of a donation than a trade, Roger was encouraged that they had come this far. "A trade," Roger said. "That's an idea."

"No trade," Louis said. "They'll need to purchase them. We'll need to get paid."

"Later, maybe we can trade," said Vernon.

All right, Roger thought—let's just move it ahead. On the other hand, he knew what it was like getting an appropriation from the government, even just a few grand for some buffalo. It could take forever. That would be a very sad irony indeed if the Taos Pueblo Indians were ready to do the deal, but the state couldn't find the dough. Roger would have to think about how to finesse it.

"They've got to be DNA-tested and healthy, though," Roger said, adding, "I'll be happy to step aside and let this thing happen." He didn't want to saddle himself with the deal; it was their circle to complete.

"No, no," Louis protested. "We want you to be part of it. You already know this Swepston fellow."

"We might even want to go see this herd," Vernon suggested.

"No problem," Roger said. In the other meeting, there had been this static of fear and resentment in the air—the interference caused by two hundred years of violence and indifference. Now it felt like they were all on the same side. It was a little too good to be true. "That would be great if you went to Texas to see the herd. You could visit the Haley Memorial Library in Midland as well, which has all Goodnight's papers. I should have remembered to bring copies of those letters with me today—the ones from your War Captain Lujan back in 'twenty-nine, thanking Goodnight for the buffalo."

Vernon turned and addressed Louis. "We need to set up a time frame to do it all before December. Before the administration changes." He flashed a knowing smile.

"That would be great," Roger said. It would be more than great. It was absolutely necessary. If they didn't get it done by December, it would be as if this meeting had never taken place at all.

On his way back to Santa Fe, Roger met his old friend John Painter for a drink at a restaurant in the foothills of the Sangre de Cristo Mountains outside of Taos. Its patio, ringed by a low white stucco wall, had a spectacular view of the valley and the Taos Gorge, along which Charles Goodnight had traveled 150 years earlier to meet Standing Deer for the first time. As the day cooled, the two men sat with their margaritas and watched the sun make its way down the sky.

"Remember the time I was visiting you with Charlie," Roger said, "and we were out in your pasture with the buffalo and the calves?"

"And Charlie had no interest in them, but one of my cows was making a troubling noise," John remembered.

"Which I noticed. She was about fifteen feet away, looking menacingly at us, and I said, 'Let me know if we're in trouble,' and you said, 'Roger, we've been in trouble for quite a while.'"

They both laughed and sipped their drinks. "So how is he?" John asked.

"Charlie couldn't be better."

"I don't think he'll get more aggressive at this point—that's one thing you don't have to worry about. He's a pretty mellow guy. Probably the mellowest bison in the history of the planet."

"I want you to look after him if I die before you, John."

"What?"

Roger put his margarita down and looked John in the eye. "It's the real reason I wanted to meet you for a drink. I wanted to look you in the eye and ask you to take care of him if something happens."

"Well, I'd be honored."

"Veryl can't handle him alone."

"I know that."

"There's no one else to do it. There's nothing more precious to me in this world, except Veryl." Roger quickly looked away toward the setting sun, bisected now by the black serrated profile of the mountains. He knew John was one of the few people who could understand that the living thing he loved second most in the world was a lame buffalo.

"I'll give him his own corral"—John too was in silhouette now—"and I'll go out there every day and we'll reminisce about what a great guy you were."

"Not so fast," Roger said, enjoying John, the sunset, the drink, his meeting with the Taos Pueblo Indians, the unexpected richness of it all. "I'm not going anywhere yet."

"I sure as hell hope not."

"But I won't last as long as Charlie."

twenty

In mid-July 2003, while Veryl was on a weeklong painting trip in the Rocky Mountains with some other artists, Roger went out to the arena to take Charlie for a hike.

As Roger approached the large rectangular arena, he didn't see Charlie right away and assumed he'd gone back to his stall. As he changed his course slightly, heading for the barn, he heard a low grumble and lifted his head. At the far end of the arena, Charlie was lying on his left side near the fence with all four legs off the ground. Roger hopped into the arena and raced to him. As he got closer, he could see that Charlie was terrified, unable to get up. In his struggles, he had kicked down part of the fence. Blood was caked in one nostril. All Roger could surmise was that he had caught his head in the fence, twisted his neck, re-injured his spine, and the pain or a muscle spasm was immobilizing him. He couldn't throw his head to the right, which meant he couldn't initiate the process of getting up. Now he lay helplessly on his side, his all-too-human right eye looking plaintively at Roger.

"Stay right there, Charlie," Roger said, his heart pounding. "I've got an idea." He went to the barn and returned with a break bar, six feet and fifty pounds of iron used for breaking up asphalt. He slipped one end of it under Charlie's neck and with both hands on the other pushed as hard as he could. If he could only leverage Charlie's head a foot or so off the ground, it might be enough for Charlie to get his legs under him. However, the only thing that moved was the break bar itself, which, unbelievably, bent under the strain.

Roger ran to the house, called the fire department from his office, and asked the dispatcher to send some men out to help him raise a hurt buffalo.

"I'm afraid that's not the kind of thing we do."

"Ma'am, I've got a very tame buffalo with an injured neck and if I don't get him up on his feet soon, the shame of it, if not the pain, is going to kill him."

"I'm sorry, sir. I can't dispatch firefighters to your house just because your buffalo is hurt. If I did that every time someone called with a hurt buffalo—"

"What do you mean, *every* time? When did you ever get a

call from someone with a buffalo before? This is an emergency, ma'am."

"Maybe you should call a vet."

"I don't need a vet right now. I need four strong men."

"Why don't you call some friends?"

"If I had four strong friends lying around, do you think I'd be calling you? Now, look, I've got a three-year-old buffalo here who's almost a member of the family, he's hurt, and I need to get him up."

"I'm very sorry, sir."

"Ma'am, has your department ever rescued a kitten from a tree?"

"I believe so."

"I rest my case."

"I'm sorry, sir?"

Roger slammed down the phone and ran out the door to the arena again, where Charlie still lay on his side, as helpless as a beached whale, nostrils dilating, kicking at the air futilely. In the barn, Kepler whinnied. Roger knelt by Charlie's side, soothing him.

"It's all right," he said, stroking his muzzle. "We'll get you back on your feet. Hang in there."

Charlie grunted. After three years, Roger could distinguish the slightest gradation of meaning in Charlie's grunts. The sound he made now was a heart-rending plea for help. Roger did the only thing he could think of—he ran back into the house and called the fire department again.

"I've got smoke in the house," he said.

"Didn't you just call about a buffalo?"

"Yeah, but now there's smoke in the house. I'm not sure if it's related."

"You're the guy with the buffalo."

"I'm the guy with smoke in my house coming from an unidentified source. You better send some men and a truck down here."

There was another pause before the dispatcher said, "All right."

"Thank you, ma'am," Roger replied. "*Thank* you."

When the three firemen arrived twenty minutes later, sirens blaring, Roger was waiting for them. They hopped off the truck and followed Roger to the scene, where the break bar and some loose boards from the barn were now lying next to Charlie. Together, the four of them tried to leverage Charlie to an upright position. Using hay bales as shims to secure their progress, they finally succeeded. Charlie was standing. Roger could see now that, in his struggles, Charlie had worn patches of hair off his flank and broken the skin in a couple of places, exposing dark red tissue underneath. But he was up.

"Thank you, gentlemen," Roger said, walking the firemen back to their truck.

"No problem," one of them replied, the sweat still pouring off his face. "Although you may want to consider a smaller pet."

"He's not a pet. He'd be with his own kind, except he's lame and couldn't survive in a herd."

"So you're stuck with him?"

"I'm not stuck in the least," Roger said, although what he was thinking was that everyone was stuck with something or someone, but not everyone was lucky enough to be stuck with a buffalo.

After the firemen left, Roger went back and walked Charlie to his stall, then called a neighbor, a veterinarian named Tom Parker, who gave Charlie some steroids to control whatever swelling there was in his neck. Charlie seemed fine the rest of the day. The next two days passed uneventfully, although the world once again felt fragile, and all the more so since Roger couldn't reach Veryl, who was incommunicado for several more days up in the Rockies. He fretted alone, checking on Charlie almost every hour.

Two mornings after the incident, before dawn, Roger went to the arena and found Charlie down again on his left side, bleeding from the nose. Roger pulled blood and mucus out of Charlie's nasal passage, then called Tom Parker and two other neighbors. After they got Charlie up with the break bar and some hay bales, the vet took Roger aside.

"You need to get this animal to some place where he can be taken care of," he said.

"I know."

"Maybe you ought to haul him back up to CSU," the vet said, "where you had him before."

"That's what I was thinking." Sherry Gaber was in Europe and he didn't feel he had much choice. Within two hours, he was on the road, dragging his sick buffalo behind him in an old borrowed horse trailer—Charlie had long outgrown their small one—in the direction of Colorado State University's School of

Veterinary Medicine. Nine long, lonely hours of blacktop and a lot of unanswered questions lay ahead of him. He pounded the heel of his hand against the steering wheel. He had thought they were out of the woods. Still, he felt some optimism brewing beneath his frustration. He was doing *something*.

The roads were bad. Nothing made you aware of it like having a hurt animal behind you. I'm on a federal highway, Roger thought, and my buffalo's getting potholed to death. It would be nice, he thought, to have some of those billions being spent in Iraq to rebuild this country's infrastructure. It would also be nice if their custom-made horse trailer had already come. "Hang in there, Charlie," he yelled over his shoulder.

Somewhere between Walsenburg and Pueblo, Colorado, the city where the young Charles Goodnight had lived before heading for Texas to make his fame and fortune in the 1870s, Roger felt a little tickle in his throat. A bubble of dread was forming, threatening to close off his airway. He tried to clear it, force it up and out of his throat. He coughed over and over again. He recognized it. A little nervous retching cough. The same one he developed whenever he was about to face a combat situation for Air America. He was doing it again, for the first time in thirty-four years.

At CSU, it was 102 degrees and things were different than they had been before. At 1,800 pounds, Charlie was more than three times the size he had been on his last visit two and a half years earlier and everybody was a little afraid of him. The veterinary students who had treated him before had moved on, and the new crop, who might have been well disposed toward Charlie had they remembered him as the valiant and personable adolescent buffalo who had beaten the odds and walked out of CSU under his own steam, regarded Charlie as simply another unpredictable large mammal to look after. The staff wouldn't enter his stall unless Roger was there, in case something happened—even though Roger knew Charlie was in no shape to hurt anybody. He was pained to see that vulnerable look in Charlie's eyes again.

Dr. Callan loaded him up with painkillers, then examined his neck. There was obvious swelling, but no definitive diagnosis. Dr. Callan proposed operating on his neck, but that again raised the issue of the dangers of anesthesia for ruminants, and this time the situation wasn't so dire that Roger was willing to risk it. Heroic measures did not seem required. What Charlie really needed, it dawned on Roger after a few days in Fort Collins, was Sherry Gaber.

He left CSU with a pocketful of antibiotics. Charlie stood in the trailer all the way back, 450 miles straight down Interstate 25 to Santa Fe. Roger wondered if he had accomplished anything at CSU. It was a wash, he decided; Charlie was no better, but at least he was no worse. At least he hoped not, as the trailer took another federal bump. The roads around Denver were the worst. Every flaw in the road had to be hell for Charlie.

Roger listened to Andy Wilkinson's songs on CD and to National Public Radio. The news out of Washington and Iraq was depressing. You couldn't blow into Iraq without an exit strategy any more than you could blow into a buffalo's pen without one. Roger was in his late fifties now and the country didn't seem to have changed much. He felt that it was in the hands of self-serving and arrogant ideologues with neither a respect for history nor a true regard for the future. He had been around a long time and he hadn't met many men who could understand the great but fragile web we were all part of and wanted to help keep it together.

What Roger felt was that there had to be a better America than this one. And maybe it was that hope that helped explain his love for the crippled beast, this symbolic survivor of nineteenth-century America, in the back of his horse trailer. It was animals who kept men honest. No amount of money or flattery—or even carrots—could get an animal to be untrue to itself. The ground on which humans, who were part animal, met animals, more human than we know, was sacred. Animals taught us to love even when we couldn't know whether we are loved back. It was there, in an animal's heartbeat, that we could feel the pulse of something bigger than we were. There, on that ground, we could feel that we were a part of nature, not apart from it.

Roger flashed on the situation in Yellowstone again. He knew that a man who didn't treat an animal with respect not only had no respect for nature; he had no respect for himself.

WHEN ROGER REACHED SANTA FE, he led Charlie down the ramp and let him graze for a minute. Charlie barely nibbled. The road-weary, thirsty buffalo shambled across the barn's brick floor toward his stall. But a hoof slipped, slid, and in an instant he was down. This time, half with Roger's help, half under his own power, Charlie managed to get to his feet. He took a few little steps and fell again just outside his stall. This

204 • R. D. ROSEN

time Roger was caught between Charlie and the stall wall. Roger saw it coming, couldn't get out of the way, and stiffened to absorb the impact. He made his body as rigid as possible as almost two thousand pounds of bison crashed into him. Being 230 pounds and a black belt in karate had never come in so handy. Charlie hit him across the middle—luckily. Had he fallen against Roger's knees, it would not have been pretty.

"That's all right, Charlie," he said, helping him back on his feet. "That's okay, buddy. It's all right."

But it wasn't okay. It was beginning to feel as if there was a glass partition between them, the way there is between the healthy and the sick. Though the ill remain like us in every way but their illness, they inhabit a different world, fragile and unreliable, separated from others by the immediacy of their pain and fear. To dissipate some of the strangeness, humans can acknowledge it in words. Roger and Charlie seemed to have reached the limits of their extraordinary intimacy. Moreover, Charlie wouldn't touch his food, which meant Roger couldn't give him the antibiotics Dr. Callan had prescribed. In his stall, Charlie lowered his head and started eating dirt. It broke Roger's heart.

"This is a life-and-death situation," he told Sherry Gaber on her return from her trip. He pressed a cold pack against the bruise on his stomach. "His atlas is tipped. I don't know what else is wrong with him, and I'm not sure *they* did either up at CSU, but he's falling again, Sherry. I need you over here. Maybe he'll listen to you."

Sherry drove over and tried to get the angle on Charlie, his lowered head almost between her legs, her hands gently on his horns to steady him. When she got close to his atlas, he protested, tossing his head. Sherry had to let go of his horns, but she stood her ground, all five feet two inches of her, nothing between them, not even fence rails, and tried again. This time Charlie tolerated it long enough for her to get her hands on that first vertebra to make a partial adjustment. But Charlie wouldn't allow any more. The neck was too sensitive.

"No sense pushing it," she told Roger. "I'll have to come back and try again later." When she returned in a few hours, Charlie was still combative. "It's your pal Sherry," Roger said, trying to calm him. Sherry almost gave up, but she talked to him and, finally, she was able to get in a good adjustment. Charlie immediately calmed down and seemed better, and hope burst open in Roger like a flower.

"I don't know what I'd do without you, Sherry," Roger said, towering over her. He coughed. It came out with three or four little bursts, like a cold car engine turning over in January.

"What's wrong? What's the cough?" she asked.

"Nothing."

Roger stayed up with Charlie in his stall until 2 A.M. that night, making sure he was comfortable, hovering anxiously, watching for signs of relapse. He stayed with Charlie in the gloom of the barn's low lights, surrounded by darkness, with the three horses shifting and snorting in the adjacent stalls. Finally, when Charlie was fast asleep, Roger crept off to his bedroom, lonelier than ever with a sick buffalo in the barn and a wife somewhere in the Rockies. He set the alarm clock for 5 A.M.; three hours of sleep was all his conscience would agree to.

When the alarm yanked him out of sleep, he dressed and walked out into the warm, inky night. "Oh, Charlie," he said at the door to his stall. He was down again on his side, the fourth time in eight days. At dawn, he called Tom Parker and his friend Jeff Stuermer and a college kid he knew, Shane Loretzen, and the three of them got Charlie up and sternal, but not before some mishaps. The break bar hit Stuermer in the head and Charlie grazed Roger's pelvis with the side of his horn, leaving a bruise that wouldn't go away for an entire year. But they finally righted him and bunkered his stall with more hay bales to prevent him from falling.

In the days that followed, Charlie's health was up and down, but with some overall improvement. When Veryl returned from the Rockies with a dozen small landscapes and a backpack full of dirty clothes, Charlie was drinking water from his black plastic tub, but he was going two or three days without eating a thing before he'd begin picking at his hay again. He stayed on his feet, though, and he began to lose the look of vulnerability Roger had noticed since Fort Collins. The distance between the two of them was again closing. Roger, who increasingly felt that the trip up to Colorado State University had been worthless, was telling friends that Sherry had saved Charlie's life.

twenty-one

Charlie appeared to be well on the way to recovery when friends from the East came to visit at the end of July 2003. He was still off his feed, but every day he ate a little something: a bit of hay, half a carrot. The friends watched in amazement as Roger entered the stall, sat down on a bale of hay, and patted it. Charlie, who had been lying sternal, immediately got to his feet in a series of movements so quick and fluid it was easy to forget the size of the animal involved, then slowly turned in the crowded space so that he was facing Roger, his head almost touching Roger's pants. Then, like some oversized pussycat,

Charlie lowered his head and began rubbing it back and forth against Roger's leg. The friends had never seen anything like it outside of an animated Disney movie.

The next day, Sherry came to adjust his atlas vertebra again and was pleased to find that he was holding the previous adjustment. Roger took Charlie for a short walk with Sherry around the arroyo on the perimeter of the property. As Charlie slowly zigged and zagged to inspect various vegetation, trampling a few plants in the process, the only visible sign of anything wrong with him was how he still hoisted his stiff hind right leg forward with each step. Roger explained to his friends that walking with Charlie was like walking with a two-year-old child; you had to allow for many distractions and a general disregard for anyone else's rhythm or timetable, then take advantage of his momentary losses of interest to motivate and redirect him. Charlie occasionally needed a literal pat on the butt to get on with it. His bad leg started to look more limber, and at one point he began trotting down the arroyo, forcing Roger to jog ahead. Then he stopped for a long pee, in which he stood happily for a moment before backing up so he could smell it.

On Sunday, August 3, a couple of days after the friends left, Roger and Veryl were watching Charlie graze in the backyard through their living room window when they noticed he was breathing rapidly. It was hot out, the high dry heat of August, but he was in the shade and his flanks were still going in and out like bellows. Roger tracked down Dr. Callan in Colorado. He told Roger to take Charlie's temperature and, if it was over 103, to give him the powdered oral antibiotic he'd prescribed for him at CSU, the one Roger hadn't been able to give him since

Charlie stopped eating. Roger called his neighbor, the vet Tom Parker, who recommended giving him an injection of antibiotics right away and started him on a seven-day course. Parker came over and the two of them tried to get Charlie under control. In his distress, though, Charlie was totally uncooperative. Parker and Roger finally tied him down in the corner of his stall with three ropes. Charlie only stopped struggling when Roger finally laid his hand on him. Even in his frenzy, he knew Roger's touch. Charlie's temperature was 102.8.

Only now did Roger glance at the label of the oral antibiotics Callan had given him; the drug was indicated for the treatment of a condition Roger had never heard of: shipping fever. What the heck was that? At CSU nobody had mentioned shipping fever. When he showed the label to Veryl, she went and Googled it.

Shipping fever got its name because it often occurs in animals that have been transported long distances. Its real name was bovine respiratory disease, its medical one pleuropneumonia, and it was often deadly. The stress of travel can decrease immune function in the lungs, but there were several purely physical factors as well. Trailers are full of respiratory irritants, including hay dust, mold spores, exhaust fumes, and the ammonia from the urine. When a horse, cow, or sheep keeps its head above chest level for several hours at a time, bacteria are given a chance to thrive in the animal's lower airways, making it hard to clear mucus and bacteria from its lungs. It's not uncommon for an animal that hasn't lowered its head for twenty-four hours to develop pneumonia. Because shipping fever costs cattle producers $600 million a year in lost livestock, veterinary medicine was desperately trying to understand the disease and develop recombinant DNA–derived vaccines to prevent it.

The early signs of shipping fever, which include mild depression, lack of interest in food, and increased respiratory rate, can become apparent during travel, but may not manifest themselves for up to two weeks. Even then, the symptoms could be very subtle.

By Wednesday, August 6, Roger thought it was premature to call Charlie recovered, but there was clear improvement. The antibiotic was doing its job. He grazed a bit on the rope lead and felt strong enough to trot along the arroyo on the property, dragging Roger after him. The next morning, he ate a very small amount of hay and straw and took a bite of carrot. By Thursday evening, Roger could see continued progress. "He's feeling good," Tom Parker said. "We'll get him through this." Veryl high-fived Roger, who hesitated for a moment to slap her hand. He was not naturally optimistic, and he didn't feel that they were in the clear yet.

On Friday, he could tell they weren't. Charlie's head was down. He put up with the shot, but he wouldn't touch food. A zoological-nutritionist friend had recommended an appetite stimulant, which Roger tried to squirt through a syringe into Charlie's mouth. He did this by lying on his back underneath him, hardly the safest place in the world to be, since in his distress Charlie would no longer let even Roger touch his head or horns.

"Open up. Just have a little."

Charlie wasn't even strong enough to grunt.

"C'mon," Roger said, poking at Charlie's closed mouth with the plastic syringe. "C'mon, now, Charlie. When you were little you wouldn't *stop* eating. You remember how you used to tap dance for more the moment you finished a bottle? And then when you weren't sucking a bottle anymore—please open up, Charlie—you ate constantly. Wiped out every flower bed. Good thing I introduced you to carrots—some days it was the only way I could get you to do anything. Open your mouth and let me squirt some of this crap in there! Charlie! I'm a fifty-nine-year-old man *lying on his back underneath a buffalo*! I'm begging you! Open your damn mouth and eat!"

Sweat poured down the sides of Roger's face. "Charlie," he said, "you've got to eat something or you're going to die."

twenty-two

Tom Parker explained to Roger that the bacteria sometimes formed a resistant ball inside the animal. Roger imagined a shaking fist of bacteria inside Charlie. He and Veryl were in crisis mode now. Roger remembered that on the phone Rob Callan had mentioned two other antibiotics that might work. Since the original one seemed to be losing its effectiveness, on Friday afternoon Roger drove an hour into Albuquerque to pick the others up at a veterinary supply store.

Charlie didn't respond to either, so on Saturday it was Veryl's turn to make the trip. Desperate, she asked everyone in the store if they had any fresh ideas. When a lady vet there suggested she try running a tube down his esophagus and feeding him some concoction she described, Veryl bought the necessary supplies. She wanted to tell the woman how much Charlie meant to her, but how do you explain to a stranger that you have a buffalo at home who's like a child to you? When she got back to the house, she put cattle feed, probiotics, electrolytes, acidophilus, vitamin B-12, and a few other ingredients into a blender. With help from a vet from Eldorado who specialized in this sort of thing—it now felt as if they'd gotten every vet in the area involved—she and Roger secured Charlie again with three ropes and got the tube down his esophagus and fed him. He was too weak to protest.

It was Veryl's turn to be pessimistic. Roger clung to hope, but still he took Veryl aside.

"Honey," he said, "we've got to think about where we're going to put him."

He paused, alarmed by what he had just said. But it was as if the words were also an insurance policy; once they were out of his mouth, he felt protected by them. The words dragged him forward into the future, but defended him against it.

"It can't be very far from the barn," he added. "He's too big."

"Next to Gwalowa," Veryl said. Gwalowa, the exceptional Arabian she had been riding when she met Roger seventeen years before, was buried just outside the arena that had been Charlie's home. "I think he would want to have another exceptional animal for company."

"It's always been one of his favorite grazing spots," Roger said.

"Superb animals sticking together," she said.

Roger called a young man who had done some work for them in the past and told him that he and his backhoe might be needed in the next day or so. It felt like another painful betrayal of Charlie—like leaving him at the Montosa Buffalo Ranch two and a half years before—but Roger was by nature and training a man who prepared for all the possibilities.

Roger and Veryl planned to go see the movie *Seabiscuit* that evening. They needed the distraction. Around dinner time, they walked Charlie around a bit outside his stall, thinking it might help clear his lungs. He walked one lap, refused to do a second, and went back to his stall, where he lay down, tongue out, breathing with difficulty. They left him there, but one or the other returned to check on him every twenty minutes. After one of her trips, Veryl told Roger that she was afraid Charlie was dying and maybe they shouldn't go to the movies.

At just that moment, the new vet from Eldorado happened to call to ask after his new patient. Roger and the vet spoke for a while and concluded that Charlie was okay. But it hardly seemed so to Veryl when she went out to the barn. She walked gingerly toward Charlie's stall, as though she were the lame one. Her heart was in her throat. She walked past her horses Toddy and Matt Dillon and looked into Charlie's stall. Charlie was in the process of shifting from lying on one side to the other. He had gotten halfway up on buckled legs—like the arms of a weightlifter unable to press a barbell—and was barely able to lower himself. "Good boy," she whispered, choked up at the thought that so much life might be sputtering to an end. But when Charlie was through settling himself, she allowed herself to find in his small achievement some cause for genuine hope.

Drained, she and Roger dragged themselves to *Seabiscuit*. From the beginning, Roger didn't want to be there, and it was all he could do to stay in his seat. Of all the movies to be seeing, why did it have to be this one, with all the parallels? The animal with the bad leg that no one had wanted, no one had understood, until a man had seen in him a big soul and special drive and, with patience, kindness, and understanding had released the champion within. It wasn't whether you finished first, or how many people were watching when you crossed the finish line, but where you had started, and how far you had come. During Seabiscuit's climactic triumph over War Admiral, Roger felt an almost unbearable sadness.

The minute they got home, a little before ten, Roger put on his boots and headed for the barn, asking Veryl to go inside the house to make some mush in the blender for Charlie. Veryl headed toward the kitchen, grim visions of intubating Charlie again in her head. But why was she letting Roger go alone? Why had Roger sent her into the house?

She stopped, hesitated, then turned back toward the barn. Before she even entered, she could hear Charlie's rapid breathing.

"He can't get air," Roger said, crouching near Charlie, who was in the sternal position. Flag, the Rottweiler, the one dog in the house with strong maternal instincts, pushed open the stall door with his nose and padded in to see what she could do.

Roger braced Charlie on either side with hay bales.

Charlie's eyes were puffy. Gone was the vulnerable look he had worn on and off since his visit to Colorado State University more than three weeks ago. In its place was a look of great ending. The life was slowly going out in his eyes now, like house lights dimming in a theater.

"He's dying," Veryl whispered to Roger. The words came out on their own, although she knew she wouldn't have said it in front of Charlie if she thought he was really there. But he wasn't; she could see that he had already left the living.

Roger felt his throat tightening and a hot pressure building behind his eyes. It was unimaginable, after everything, that Charlie would leave him now. He was supposed to outlive all of them, to go on and on, to have been a gift for Roger and Veryl to leave behind to others. How could any creature with so large a heart and so fierce a desire to live just slip away? Roger thought they had had a deal, and this was not part of it. For a moment, Roger was as numb as a child, all raw wordless hurt and no understanding.

The buffalo, lying sternal with his forelegs folded neatly under his chest, shuddered once. As the air in his lungs escaped for the last time, it came out as a bellow that made him, for an instant, seem entirely alive again. Then his head fell forward and he died.

It took Roger a moment to catch up to the reality of it. It felt like he was running after him again, down the arroyo, except that when he caught up, Charlie was no longer there.

Roger reached over and gently closed Charlie's eyes one at a time and it was as if Charlie were sleeping, except for the fact that his nose touched the ground.

❧

THE NEXT DAY, the young man with the backhoe came and went about his business quickly and quietly. Because of the heat, Charlie needed to be put to rest without delay. Roger didn't want Veryl to see any of it, the digging of the grave or the indignity of Charlie being picked up in the backhoe's bucket and carried across the arena, through the gate, and over to his final place. He buried Charlie next to Gwalowa, and tossed a few carrots in with Charlie before the backhoe finished its work, and then he arranged some rocks in the letter C to mark the spot. That evening, Veryl went out to the arena alone and raked over the backhoe tracks. Roger got into his truck and went out in search of a soccer game.

twenty-three

The next day, August 11, 2003, Roger and Veryl e-mailed everyone who had known and loved Charlie. "Charlie died last night," their letter began. "Veryl and I were holding him. He was buried this morning in his pasture." The e-mail's subject line read: "With The Herd." Soon, the calls, cards, e-mails, flowers, and plants started pouring in. Some friends had been moved to flights of Western poetry: "We are so sorry to hear Charlie has gone to the big long grass prairie in the sky"; "I'm sure enough tears have fallen to water his pasture"; "Love is the only gift we can give someone which they can take with them when they die. Charlie was probably the most well-loved buffalo ever to make it into bison heaven." Most, though, simply expressed the sentiments that people whose lives are not spent with animals might find embarrassing, if not incomprehensible: "I hated to read that e-mail and have shed tears of love and loss for Charlie. . . . He brought out the best in many people (especially you two) and has left a huge legacy. We truly loved him and I will always remember his eyes, entire beauty and huge, eternal spirit"; "Helping him cross over to what lies ahead is the most precious gift anyone can give to another. What a privilege it has been for you both."

Veryl had never seen Roger so emotional. When Charlie had gotten hurt, Roger had slipped back easily into the caregiver's role. But it hadn't been the same role as before, because Charlie was suddenly a diminished animal dependent on Roger for having any kind of life at all. In the time it took a scared buffalo to crash into a metal fence, Roger had gone from being an obsolete parent of a lovable baby bison to a starring role in a drama about the outer limits of human friendship with a wild animal. Veryl didn't think he had ever given his heart so fully to anyone or anything—even her. When she had met Roger, he was a forty-three-year-old bachelor, inexperienced in love. He had given her more than he had given anyone before, yet there was a piece she knew he had given only to Charlie.

She did not feel slighted. If anything, she was jealous— jealous of the relationship's intensity not because it left her out, but because *she* had never had a relationship with an animal to match it. She had loved so many animals herself, but none had demanded of her what Roger had willingly given to Charlie. She had buried a lot of animals and never known anything like it. Yet she alone truly knew what Roger had lost. Ethologists and philosophers argue endlessly about what animals feel, and whether they feel in the same way that humans do. In Charlie's case, Veryl understood, it was a question of something else altogether: how deeply an animal can get a human to feel.

In the weeks after Charlie's death, Roger would remember how sweet and clean Charlie smelled, like laundry fresh out of the dryer, and how he would pull out a tuft of Charlie's woolly hair and hold it up to someone's nose, as if to say that things in the world were not at all what you thought they were. And Roger would worry that he would never smell anything like it again. He would think of the phase when Charlie was getting too big to be left alone in the backyard because he might eat a small tree or get into an argument with a lawn chair. But most of all, he would think about what it was like to walk out the door in the Santa Fe morning, head down to the arena, and see this majestic animal waiting for you, and to touch him, and know that he was your friend.

Self-reproach compounded Roger's suffering. He saw all his mistakes in retrospect. He shouldn't have kept Charlie so isolated from other animals. He should have gotten Charlie up to John Painter at the Montosa Buffalo Ranch earlier in the day, given him more daylight to get accustomed to the other buffalo. Why had he hauled Charlie up to CSU in all that heat right after he'd reinjured himself a few weeks before? Why couldn't the new horse trailer have been ready, so that Charlie could have had a more comfortable ride? Why hadn't he installed a squeeze chute in his pen to make it easier to treat him?

Roger turned these thoughts over and over in his mind,

even though it probably made more sense to ask how a man who had never been anywhere near bison before could nurse a gravely injured buffalo back to some facsimile of health. It made more sense to ask how he could care for him day after day. It made more sense to ask how he taught a buffalo to follow instructions. It made more sense to ask how an animal who shouldn't have been able to walk again learned to run. It made more sense to ask why the buffalo had survived at all, and whether he had survived, despite the pain, just to be with Roger.

Roger funneled some of his grief into anger at President Bush's administration. "Iraq is a tar pit and should always have been recognized as such," he wrote in a letter to the editor of the *New Mexican*. "In the lead-up to the war, the administration spewed vastly inaccurate propaganda to a frightened public. . . . The U.S. Senate, the body whose most important responsibility is to declare war, was reduced to a well-dressed group of eunuchs by the totally political timing of the war resolution, putting the power of war in the hands of only one man." Roger ended with a flourish that invoked the buffalo jumps of the past: "We have no energy policy unless it is attacking an oil-rich nation, no balanced environmental policy, no clue as to how to revive the economy and no one to resist the steamrollering of the average American by 'conservative' special interests. If this is the direction we want to be led, then there's a big cliff in our future."

The Taos Pueblo Indians, who had seemed so interested at the most recent meeting in giving, trading, or selling a few bison to Goodnight's old herd in Texas, never followed up that fall. When the administration changed at the end of 2003, Roger would once again defer his dream about a ceremonial transfer of bison attended by the Indians and the governors of both New Mexico and Texas.

To provide Roger with a sense of purpose in the weeks after Charlie's death, Veryl suggested they take a trip up to Yellowstone to investigate the situation there, which was frustratingly complex. Any solution would somehow have to balance the interests of a broad spectrum of parties: Montana cattle ranchers, the Montana Department of Livestock, the Montana Department of Fish, Wildlife, and Parks, the U.S. Departments of Agriculture and the Interior, Congress, the National Park Service, Native American groups, the Buffalo Field Campaign, the National Forest Service, a group of homeowners just outside of Yellowstone who love seeing the buffalo in their neighborhood in late winter and early spring, and assorted environmentalists and wildlife conservationists. At one extreme, there were those who wanted to see wild buffalo herds return to till and revitalize the prairie; at the other were ranchers and farmers to whom the buffalo remained an unwanted nemesis from—and often unconscious reminder of—the past. As one Montana Department of Livestock agent said after 230 buffalo wandering in Yellowstone had been captured just inside the park and slaughtered without testing in 2001–2, "Let's kill all the bison. There aren't any real Indians left, anyway."

VERYL TELEPHONED the Buffalo Field Campaign, whose headquarters is a rambling communal log house outside West Yellowstone. A volunteer named Justine Sanchez, a housewife and mother from Colorado, answered and listened as Veryl talked about Charlie and how much she and her husband wanted to fly up to spend a day in Yellowstone. Justine in turn called Dan Brister at his summer home in Missoula, Montana, and recounted her conversation with Veryl. Brister, who had just completed a master's thesis on the history of the buffalo, recognized the Goodnight name immediately and remembered that three of his bison had helped seed the Yellowstone herd. Brister decided to drive the 250 miles from Missoula to Yellowstone just to show these folks around.

Early one morning toward the end of August, Roger's Cessna Conquest started its descent into West Yellowstone. He glanced to his left, in the direction of Charlie's birthplace. When they touched down at the small airport, it was barely seven in the morning and their plane's engines were the only thing that broke the silence. Climbing out of the plane, Roger and Veryl had the feeling that they were entering the next stage of an unexpected journey that had taken them into the past and was now leading them into the future.

Dan Brister and Justine Sanchez were waiting for them. After breakfast in West Yellowstone, Dan drove them toward Hayden Valley, the heart of the park's bison range. On either side of the road, fallen spruce, fir, and pine from the great fires of 1988 littered the hillsides like Pick Up Stix. In the car, Dan decried the institutionalized bias against the buffalo, the intricacies of the different agencies they were fighting. When Dan started asking questions about their experience with Charlie, Veryl had to do all the answering because Roger was still too emotional to talk about it.

Dan suddenly pulled the car over to the side of the road, and it took Roger and Veryl a moment to see why. There, across the river, shrouded in the steam of a thermal seep, were thirty or forty buffalo. The four of them got out of the car and stood on the riverbank, watching. It was the very end of rutting season and some of the bulls were wallowing, still advertising their impressive testosterone levels. One bull was tending a cow, making sure other suitors kept their distance. Two other bulls squared off to decide their pecking order in the reproductive dance. Another big bull cruised slowly through the herd, sniffing cows, working the room. An assortment of calves, their coats honey or russet or brown, wandered like contented children at a family picnic. But most of the buffalo stood stock still, seeming less like animals than bits of the inanimate landscape—outcroppings of rock and huge clods of earth. The scene, softened by the seep, had a mystical quality, like something only imagined.

As he watched the proceedings on the other side of the river, Roger felt a brief surge of relief. The sight of the buffalo, the progeny of those few animals who had escaped through the cracks of a nightmare 130 years before, delivered him for a moment from his mourning. Charlie had walked into his life, told his story, and then disappeared, but the story, and these buffalo, were still alive, and the gift was still in motion.

EPILOGUE

A few months after Charlie's death, Roger began investigating in earnest the conflict surrounding the Yellowstone buffalo. He brought to it the same intensity, sense of justice, and gift for compromise that he brought to everything he took up—and the conflict increasingly seemed to need someone with the last trait. The winter of 2003–4 brought the worst killing of Yellowstone buffalo—281 in all—since 1996–97, when the slaughter of over one thousand bison first forced the issue out in the open and spurred the founding of the Buffalo Field Campaign.

In the summer of 2004, when the pain of Charlie's death had started to fade, Roger flew back to Yellowstone to attend a three-day seminar on the history and biology of bison, given at the Yellowstone Institute in the Lamar Valley. He also met with the Buffalo Field Campaign's founder and executive director, Mike Mease, who walked him past the Duck Creek capture facility just west of Yellowstone, where DOL agents rounded up migrating buffalo, only occasionally tested them, and sent them on to slaughter. That same day, Roger spent a couple of hours with Karrie Taggart of Horse Butte Neighbors of the Buffalo (HOBNOB), a group of pro-buffalo homeowners in one of the public land areas outside of Yellowstone where the park's bison migrated in spring. She spoke of how much she enjoyed seeing the buffalo grazing in their neighborhood in the spring, and how little she appreciated the DOL hazing that went on in her own front yard.

Roger had lunch at a West Yellowstone café with the National Park Service's Rick Wallen, a bison biologist at Yellowstone who was disturbed by the fate of the bison and the cattle industry's entrenched opposition to the animal. "Elk have all the rights of wildlife species," he told Roger, "but buffalo are managed like livestock. We worry that even if we solved the brucellosis problem, they'd [the Montana Department of Livestock] still go after the buffalo. But Wyoming is not a zoo. The bison need land outside of the park as a vital part of their natural habitat." The area's cattle ranchers, Wallen told Roger, "could make the income they needed through conservation easements"—taking federal and often state tax credits for putting private land in public trust so it will remain natural and undeveloped. Wallen praised the Buffalo Field Campaign for forcing the Montana Department of Livestock "to be accountable," but complained that the group failed "to support any feasible solution."

Three months later, things began to look up. In November of 2004, the Buffalo Field Campaign hailed the election of Democrat Brian Schweitzer as the new governor of Montana, sharing their enthusiasm on their website: "Governor-elect Schweitzer has expressed his disdain for the way things are going now, and we look to him to keep his word and put a stop to the atrocious treatment of the buffalo. . . . Schweitzer, a farmer and rancher, said that management should be guided by 'science, not hyperbole,' and that the DOL is 'ill-equipped to manage buffalo in Montana.' "

Shortly after Schweitzer's victory, Roger wrote to Dr. Thomas Linfield, Montana's state veterinarian, introducing himself merely as "someone researching the issues concerning the bison herds of Yellowstone National Park." Among other questions directed at the contradictions in Montana's bison management policy, Roger suggested to Linfield that Montana had not lived up to its 2000 commitment to start vaccinating Yellowstone bison against brucellosis, and he asked why the Montana Department of Livestock continued to slaughter male bison, even though the Greater Yellowstone Interagency Brucellosis Committee, the Jackson [Wyoming] Brucellosis Symposium, and the National Research Council had all concluded that male bison do not constitute a brucellosis transmission threat. Why had Montana taken no steps to reduce the brucellosis in other migrating wildlife, such as elk? Linfield stonewalled.

It was obvious that a great deal of diplomacy was going to be necessary. The political and wildlife management issues were complex, and so were the jurisdictional ones; at least five state and federal agencies, all jockeying for position, were involved in the federally funded Interagency Bison Management Plan. But the real and invisible enemy was the increasing defensiveness of a vanishing culture. Between 1987, the year Frank and Deborah Popper formulated the idea of the Buffalo Commons to revitalize the Plains States ecologically and financially, and 2002, almost two-thirds of those states' counties declined in population. In fact, the cattle industry, whose exaggerated fear of brucellosis was the chief animus against the Yellowstone buffalo, was itself a vanishing proposition. Most of Montana's total cattle production—about 2.5 percent of the nation's beef—is in the eastern part of the state, far from Yellowstone, and much of that production is subsidized by American taxpayers. In seventeen Western states, according to a nine-month investigation by the *San Jose Mercury News* in 1999, the cattle industry is propped up by more than $100 million a year in taxpayer subsidies; in those states, livestock grazes on 254 million acres of national forests and federal land—an area equal to California, Oregon, Washington, and Idaho put together—at a subsidized cost of about one-tenth the grazing fee for private land. This remarkable discount is enjoyed by "Rolex ranchers," like the hotel mogul Barron Hilton and the brewing company Anheuser-Busch, for whom cattle are Western windowdressing, not business.

In any case, as the *San Jose Mercury News* investigation says, "It's not as if the Americans need the meat. Only 3.8 percent of the nation's beef cattle graze on federal lands."

Cattle, unlike buffalo, graze land to death. They are environmentally unfriendly in the extreme, especially in dry Western states. As John Morning, the director of watershed protection for an environmental group called Forest Guardians, put it in the *Mercury News*, "One very small, politically powerful industry is destroying our land. But the salt in the wound is that we're paying them to do it." Thomas Power, a University of Montana economist, called it "cowboy socialism. It's a romantically based, phony attempt to protect something from the past that no longer exists." And in the process, one might add, *killing* something from the past—buffalo—that still does.

Working in the shadows, Roger continued trying to plot a middle ground where the State of Montana and the cattle interests could save face and the buffalo could save their hides. Although he admired and supported the Buffalo Field Campaign, which continued its tireless protection of the Yellowstone bison and invaluable surveillance of the Montana DOL, Roger was troubled by the group's inflexibility on the issues. The BFC repudiated the brucellosis threat as a legitimate issue. It opposed all schemes to vaccinate the buffalo, on the grounds that any vaccination would compromise the buffalo's wildness. It envisioned expanded rangeland for the buffalo.

Increasingly, Roger felt like a solitary realist caught between intractable idealists and cattle-culture fundamentalists. On Thanksgiving Day, 2004, he wrote to Mike Mease: "I totally support the BFC and consider you to be heroes. . . . However, I don't feel that all BFC positions will help you to achieve the goals you desire. While it would be wonderful to turn back the clock and allow bison to reclaim their historical range, it isn't going to happen. . . . Brucellosis is both an issue and an excuse for Montana's cattle ranchers. . . . To weaken [the other side's] hand, we must move in the direction of reducing the incidence of brucellosis in the herd to where their brucellosis arguments simply lose credibility." Mease didn't respond. Roger pressed onward, determined to focus on, and find funding for, the search for a bison-specific brucellosis vaccine and more accurate "non-kill" screening tests.

Meanwhile, despite the new Montana governor's stated

preference for science over hyperbole, over the winter of 2004–5 the Montana legislature was cooking up even more ways to demonize the Yellowstone bison. The House proposed putting the cattle-friendly U.S. Department of *Agriculture* in charge of the Yellowstone buffalo and the eradication of brucellosis, while the Senate introduced a mind-boggling bill that would neuter all buffalo leaving Yellowstone, then ship them to Indian reservations to *start new herds with them*. Even the bill's sponsor recognized its absurdity, yet it passed its third reading in the Senate and was sent to the House in February 2005.

In the United States Congress, the Yellowstone buffalo had found more friends, but not quite enough of them. A bipartisan amendment to the Department of Interior Appropriations Bill to "prohibit the use of funds to kill bison, or assist in the killing of bison, in the Yellowstone National Park herd" lost two years in a row, by twenty-one and thirteen votes. On May 18, 2005, the authors of that failed amendment, Representative Maurice Hinchey (D–NY) and Representative Charles Bass (R–NH)—as always, the buffalo had to look to the Northeast for support—introduced the Yellowstone Buffalo Preservation Act. It sought to end the hazing, capturing, and killing of Yellowstone bison, to expand their range outside the park, and to restore sole jurisdiction inside the park to the National Park Service.

Around that time, however, a couple of things happened to prove that Montana's campaign against the Yellowstone bison had grown sufficiently reckless that it was no longer a threat to animals alone. On May 6, 2005, just after midnight, a semi-tractor trailer carrying twenty-two tons of peat moss hit a small herd of bison crossing Highway 191 a few miles outside of West

Yellowstone. During daylight hours, road signs and volunteers from the Buffalo Field Campaign alerted drivers at bison crossings, but at night it was a different story. The buffalo that Montana DOL agents had hazed back into the park during the day had predictably recrossed the highway at night—this time almost invisibly—to return to federal lands in Horse Butte and near Hebgen Lake. The driver wasn't hurt, but the collision killed six bison, whose corpses lay scattered over the highway.

The second thing that happened was that the Buffalo Field Campaign took a clear photo of a private helicopter, chartered to the Animal and Plant Health Inspection Service, hazing buffalo at an illegal altitude of roughly thirty-five or forty feet, in flagrant violation of federal air regulations. Roger began writing letters and sending the photo to the Federal Aviation Administration and the Senate Aviation Subcommittee, and, although it would take another year, the Flight Standards District Office in Helena finally got the message.

By June 2005, Roger had at last done enough research and amassed enough evidence to sit down and compose a long letter to Governor Brian Schweitzer of Montana. It was almost exactly five years since Charlie had first come into his life, almost two since he had left it. Roger identified himself in the letter as "neither a cattle rancher nor an environmental activist," but simply as "an individual who has but one objective: to do what I can to facilitate a resolution to the Yellowstone bison brucellosis issue." In one measured paragraph after another, Roger put the brucellosis threat in correct scientific perspective, but did not dismiss it; he encouraged the governor to help fund research into more advanced testing methods; he advocated commonsense solutions like restricting grazing in the contested areas to steers; and he advised returning bison management to the appropriate wildlife agency. "If you wish to quickly solve most of Montana's bison-related public relations difficulty, this management change should be a top consideration."

The letter ended with a few more forcefully delivered points. Regarding the DOL's chartered helicopter, he wrote, "I must caution you that some of these operations have been conducted in a dangerous and clearly illegal manner, well within the prohibitions contained in Federal Aviation Regulation §91.13, *Careless and Reckless Operation*. The State of Montana has no right to endanger lives and property on the ground, nor condone the dangerous and illegal operation of aircraft." As for the deaths of bison crossing Highway 191, he told the governor, "I am certain you agree that Montana cannot put human lives at risk by overprotecting a few cattle. But that is exactly what Montana is doing."

"Thank you for taking the time to consider my suggestions," he concluded. ". . . I wish you the wisdom to resolve this issue in the best interests of all concerned, which includes the bison of Yellowstone National Park.

"Sincerely, Roger Brooks."

He printed out the final version and signed it. He dropped his pebble in the pool. He'd give the governor a couple of days before sending copies of the letter to the Montana media. The governor, he thought, would almost certainly have to act on the last two points. In any case, the governor would have to wonder who this guy was, a man with no apparent affiliation, this guerrilla fighter in the war to save the Yellowstone bison, taking rather deadly aim at Montana's irrationality from his hiding place.

While Roger waited for a reply, during the winter of 2005–6, 970 Yellowstone bison were killed by state and federal agents, more than the total number killed there during the previous eight years combined. Another forty died when the state of Montana authorized its first buffalo hunt in fifteen years. It held a lottery to award fifty licenses to kill fifty bison that had wandered outside Yellowstone. To make it more challenging than the previous hunt, guides would no longer lead hunters right up to the buffalo. One license winner from Billings added a challenge of his own: for the hunt he bought an 1895 Winchester rifle, the same type of gun once used by Teddy Roosevelt, and insisted on hunting on horseback, just like the old days. Nonetheless, Joe Gutkowski, a man once named by *Field & Stream* magazine as the toughest man in the west, complained that the hunt was "still another parklike hunt," adding, "I want to see them allow these buffalo to migrate all over public land."

GUTKOWSKI'S RHETORIC ASIDE, by 2007 organizations such as the new American Bison Society, the American Prairie Foundation, the Great Plains Restoration Council, and the World Wildlife Fund were all committed to reintroducing bison to economically depressed areas of the Great Plains. An August 2007 *USA Today* cover story cited the earlier-than-scheduled arrival of "The Buffalo Common." However, there was still little to cheer about in Yellowstone. The winter of 2006–7 witnessed the slaughter of only 60 bison, but that was 60 too many considering the largely phantom issue of brucellosis, as well as the available buffalo grazing land in and around the national park. In Washington, D.C., the office of Representative Maurice Hinchey (D–NY) was retooling its legislative efforts to concentrate on the federal government's purchase of grazing rights for bison in the greater Yellowstone area.

In 2006, Roger and Veryl said good-bye to Santa Fe and Charlie's remains and moved to Colorado, where Roger continued his efforts to help the Yellowstone bison. As Christmas 2007 approached, it had been almost two and a half years since Roger sent off his letter to Governor Schweitzer and the media, and he had not heard back from anyone. He took a deep breath and, like a buffalo in a snowstorm, he put his head down and kept moving forward.

For more information on the Yellowstone buffalo situation:

Roger Brooks
Rogerandcharlie@aol.com

The Buffalo Field Campaign
PO Box 957
West Yellowstone, MT 59758
(406) 646-0070
(406) 646-0071 fax
buffalofieldcampaign.org

Ms. Suzanne Lewis, Superintendent
Yellowstone National Park
PO Box 168
Yellowstone National Park, WY 82190
(307) 344-2002
suzanne_lewis@nps.gov

Governor Brian A. Schweitzer
Office of the Governor
Montana State Capitol Building
PO Box 200801
Helena, MT 59620-0801
(406) 444-1311
(406) 444-5529 fax

For more information on the restoration of the Great Plains:

Great Plains Restoration Council
PO Box 1206
Fort Worth, TX 76101
(817) 838-9022
greatplains@gprc.org

AUTHOR'S NOTE

My introduction to Charlie the buffalo occurred in a series of suspiciously unlikely circumstances. I had been set up on a blind date in New York City with a woman who also—the matchmakers involved had failed to realize this—grew up in Chicago and knew the starting lineup of the 1969 Chicago Cubs. That coincidence was only the beginning. On our first date, I mentioned the one person I knew who had graduated from her school—a woman who had dated one of my brothers.

"She used to be my sister-in-law," Ellen said.

Then it turned out that we lived on the same block without knowing it. It was surprising that our parents had never met, since they shared some very good friends and moved in the same large circle. In fact, it's possible, my father says, that in the late 1940s he sold some fabric to Ellen's father's window-display manager.

Before long I was in Santa Fe, where Ellen's parents spent part of the year. At a small cocktail party there, I was introduced to Sherry Gaber, a friend of Ellen's parents who also happens to hail from Chicago. When she told me that she was a chiropractor for large animals, I asked, "So who's your most unusual client?" When she replied, "A lame buffalo," I said, "*That* I would love to see." Within the hour, I was at the home of Veryl Goodnight and Roger Brooks (whose birthday, it would turn out, I happen to share), being licked by a buffalo with a limp. It was exciting, but by the time Charlie's drool had dried, I had already filed it away under Unusual Animal Experiences, along with the time many years ago when I absentmindedly put my hand into a cage at the San Diego Zoo and beckoned to what I thought was a big dog, but which turned out to be a small bear, who promptly gashed the back of my hand.

I didn't give the buffalo another thought until a few days later, when I woke up preoccupied with the notion that, however extraordinary being licked by a buffalo had been, there was something even more remarkable about that visit. Certainly, Charlie's sheer size and unexpectedly gentle disposition had impressed me. I was also moved by Roger's obvious devotion to an injured animal. More subliminally, I think I saw in Roger's affinity for a buffalo a warped reflection of my own midlife struggles. In any case, something in their novel and vaguely haunting situation—a middle-aged man caring for an injured buffalo with a woman descended, as it were, from one of the saddest dramas in American history—kept calling to me. I waited until a decent hour, called Roger and Veryl, and invited myself over to talk about how I wanted to write about Charlie and their experience with him.

That afternoon found me on their patio, surrounded by a couple of overly attentive dogs, hoping to insinuate myself into the lives of Roger, Veryl, and Charlie—three creatures I barely knew. I had no reason to expect that Roger and Veryl would agree to open up their lives to me, a stranger and non-Westerner to boot. My career as a writer had wound its way through many media and genres without once touching subject matter involving anything west of the Mississippi. So I was surprised by Roger's and Veryl's blind faith in me. Perhaps they noticed, as their dogs crowded around me, that I like animals and that was good enough for them. Whatever their reason, they believed me when I told them there might be a book in their story. We then shook hands, forming one of the more rewarding and unusual collaborations I have ever known.

A WORD ABOUT the way this book was written. America is a culture where the line between fiction and reality has disappeared completely in a blaze of moral dishonesty and technological gimmickry. We live in a circus of ambiguous forms and manipulated meanings. Infotainment or docudrama? Newsertainment or entertainalism? Reality programs or programmed reality? Weapons of mass destruction or weapons of mass deception? In a climate as cynical as this, it hardly seems worth making distinctions anymore.

Nonetheless, here goes. Every contemporary event described in this book was based either on direct observation or on the memories and reconstruction of those involved. I can't vouch for the absolute accuracy of the many historical accounts I relied upon, but I trust that any errors or embellishments on the part of these sources were minor and/or unintentional. Conversations in this book have been held, inevitably, to a slightly lower standard. Some conversations were observed firsthand and recorded. Some were reconstructed from bits and pieces of firsthand accounts—occasionally with additional dialogue created in the spirit of their reality. Others were taken verbatim from videotape of Roger, Veryl, Charlie, and friends. Roger's "conversations" with Charlie were created from a combination of observing how Roger actually talked to Charlie, Roger's descriptions of events, and the odd exchange invented for dramatic effect.

—R. D. Rosen

ACKNOWLEDGMENTS

The history of the buffalo in this country has been recounted, recorded, and analyzed in great breadth and depth. I have stood shamelessly on the shoulders of many excellent books to see the vista, educate myself, and understand the context of Charlie's story. I am indebted to these books and their authors: David Dary's *The Buffalo Book: The Full Saga of the American Animal* (Sage Books, 1974); Francis Haines's *The Buffalo: the Story of American Bison and Their Hunters from Prehistoric Times to the Present* (Thomas Y. Crowell, 1970); J. Evetts Haley's *Charles Goodnight: Cowman and Plainsman* (University of Oklahoma Press, 1936); and Dale F. Lott's *American Bison: A Natural History* (University of California Press, 2002).

A number of other sources proved valuable: Montie Goodin's unpublished Charles Goodnight monologues; Veryl Goodnight's unpublished account of Charles Goodnight's experience with the buffalo; Margaret Schmidt Hacker's *Cynthia Ann Parker: The Life and the Legend* (Texas Western Press, 1990); John (Fire) Lame Deer's and Richard Erdoes's *Lame Deer, Seeker of Visions* (Washington Square Press, 1976); Anne Matthews's *Where the Buffalo Roam: Restoring America's*

Great Plains (University of Chicago Press, 1992); J. Wright Mooar's *Buffalo Days* (State House Press, 2005); *Brucellosis in the Greater Yellowstone Area* by the National Research Council (National Academy Press, 1998); Bill Neeley's *The Last Comanche Chief: The Life and Times of Quanah Parker* (John Wiley & Sons, Inc., 1995); "Depth Report 28: Back From Oblivion" (October 1997), one of the annual undergraduate publications of the College of Journalism and Mass Communications at the University of Nebraska–Lincoln; "The Giveaway of the West: A *Mercury News* Special Report," by Paul Rogers and Jennifer Lafleur, *San Jose Mercury News,* November 7, 1999; Dan Brister's unpublished manuscript, *In the Presence of Buffalo: Working to Stop the Yellowstone Slaughter;* the original transcripts of Charles Goodnight's accounts to his second wife, Corinne Goodnight, titled "Our First Entrance Into The Palo Duro Canyon," "My Remembrance Of And What I Know About Buffalo," and "Acquaintance With Standing Deer"; Andy Wilkinson's one-man play *Charles Goodnight's Last Night;* Dan O'Brien's *Buffalo for the Broken Heart: Restoring Life to a Black Hills Ranch* (Random House, 2002); Ruth Rudner's *A Chorus of Buffalo* (Marlowe & Company, 2000); and Nancy Wood's *Taos Pueblo* (Knopf, 1989).

For sharing their time, insight, and, in some cases, their food, I want to thank Richard Archuleta; Dan Brister; Dr. Rob Callan; Sherry Gaber; Montie and Emery Goodin of Goodnight, Texas; Jim Bradshaw and Pat McDaniel of the Nita Stewart Haley Memorial Library in Midland, Texas; John Painter of the Montosa Buffalo Ranch; Ninia Ritchie of the JA Ranch;

Danny Swepston; Judy Strittmatter; and Jim Garry and Harold Picton of the Yellowstone Institute.

I can't say enough about how much my comrade and crony Stephen Molton has meant to this book, spiritually and editorially. Fellow Bad Boys Harry Prichett and Rob Battles provided unbelievable friendship, genius, and laughter. (Harry: I should have known you would be the one to come up with the title!) Jarid Manos of the Great Plains Restoration Council took time off from fighting the war to preserve and revitalize the plains to improve this book and my awareness. My friends Tom Friedman, Charles Dawe, Daniel Katz, Peter Lewis, Suzie Bolotin, Antonia Fusco, Brianne Leary, Janine Jaquet, Gina Barnett, and Andy Wilkinson all pitched in with their valuable time and valued advice. My good friend and teacher in the art of enjoyment, Simon Gavron, whom I so deeply miss, provided both support and the perfect suggestion for how to begin this book. Thank you all for keeping your gifts in motion.

Many thanks go to David McCormick for representing this book loyally and well, and my great gratitude goes to Ellen Reeves, who is every writer's dream: an editor with a fine mind, an exquisite ear, and a judicious pen. She is that surprisingly rare commodity, someone who knows how to make a book better. I've been just as lucky with my publishers, and the many committed, caring people who helped bring Charlie's story to a wider audience: Ellen Adler, Jessica Colter, Sarah Fan, and Diane Wachtell at The New Press, and Porscha Burke at Random House.

Finally, thanks to Roger Brooks and Veryl Goodnight, in so

many ways my co-authors, for opening their lives and hearts to me; to Audrey and Norman Lewis, for supplying hospitality and the introduction to Charlie; to my parents, who, like the buffalo, know how to survive; and to Lucy and Isabel—my very own, and very remarkable, herd.

A Buffalo in the House

R. D. Rosen

A Reader's Guide

A Conversation with R. D. Rosen, Roger Brooks,
and Veryl Goodnight

R. D. Rosen: Do you remember your reaction when, having just met you, I asked your permission to write a book about you and Charlie? I sensed right away that your story was at the center of a much bigger web of personal and historical issues. I was deeply struck, as a writer, by the fact that you, Veryl, were descended from two people instrumental in saving all American buffalo from extinction—and here you two were, saving a single buffalo. Were you surprised by my interest? You were both always extremely supportive and cooperative, but did you have any moments of doubt or regret that you hid from me?

Roger Brooks: Other than wanting the best possible life for Charlie, my goal for him was to be an ambassador for his species. So few people have the opportunity to touch a bison, be licked by one, to smell one (very sweet and clean), and to better understand what this animal is about. I supported your writing a book because it was an extension of Charlie's ambassador role, to create a better understanding and a greater appreciation of these magnificent animals and their tragic role in America's history.

Veryl Goodnight: I wasn't surprised when you asked to write a story about Charlie. The moment I began researching the role that Charles and Mary Ann Goodnight played in saving bison from hide hunters in the 1870s, I recognized it as an untold story that needed to be written.

RDR: I certainly knew next to nothing about the buffalo's embattled history before starting to write *A Buffalo in the House*—and I was stunned by the scale of the slaughter and the widespread indifference to it. How much were you two aware of that history while raising Charlie?

Roger: I had never given the history of the bison-human encounter much thought. I gained great insight as to how inappropriately this animal was treated by white settlers and often by Indians as well. My education was the nexus for my desire to have Charlie help educate others.

Veryl: I was aware of the massive slaughter of the bison, but I was not aware of the individuals such as Charles and Mary Ann Goodnight, who devoted so much of their lives to helping bring the bison back from the brink of extinction. The story of humanity at its best inspired me to sculpt *Back from the Brink*. Why not inspire a writer too?

RDR: Has your relationship with your other animals—your horses, dogs, and cat—changed as a result of your experience with Charlie?

Roger: No.

Veryl: I have always had—and always will have—a deep love for all animals.

RDR: While writing the book, I was concerned with balancing the telling of the "small" story in the present with the "big" story in the past to which it was connected through your ancestors, Veryl. I wanted readers to see how your and Roger's love for Charlie occurred in a much larger context. I think we all struggle to see how events in our daily lives are shaped, and given meaning, by the past. I'm wondering what message you hope the book has for readers.

Roger: The book was yours to write, to interpret history and events in the way you felt as being most appropriate. Respect for the animal world is a key message in the book.

Veryl: The story of our raising Charlie was a catalyst to tell a much bigger story. The heart of the book, to me, is how such a magnificent animal was brought so close to extinction and how individuals such as Charles and Mary Ann Goodnight saw beyond the politics of the time and fought to stop the slaughter and save the remnant herds. The grand finale is telling how this history of slaughter is being repeated as the only wild and unmanaged bison herd in America, the Yellowstone herd, attempt their annual migration to lower country to calve.

RDR: What kind of feedback from your families, friends, and colleagues have you received since the book's publication? Veryl, have you gotten any interesting requests for artwork since *A Buffalo in the House* was first published?

Veryl: I have been very pleased with everyone's response to *A Buffalo in the House*. While "anything for art" is what started this chapter in our lives, the book shares our relationship with animals that supercedes their roles as models for sculpture.

RDR: You provided an e-mail address for readers to reply with their thoughts on the book. So far, what similarities are you finding in those responses?

Roger: Almost every e-mail response I received from readers had two common elements—they laughed and they cried. They also better understood that bison are not mere lumps on the prairie; they are sensitive and stoic animals that have only suffered from self-serving human attitudes.

Veryl: Roger has responded to every e-mail and read the most poignant ones to me. It seems that Charlie has helped take bison out of the realm of a "statistic" and given them a personality. Flipper did this for dolphins. And many other individual animals have done the same for their species.

RDR: At the end of *A Buffalo in the House,* Roger, you'd become an advocate for the conservation of American buffalo populations and for the fair treatment of the wild buffalo of Yellowstone National Park. What are the biggest challenges facing the buffalo population today and what kind of success have you had in drawing attention to them?

Roger: With reference only to wild bison and specifically the Yellowstone herds, they are caught between polar opposites, environmentalists and ranchers. This leaves a lot of room to develop a middle ground that recognizes the vital interests of both parties and an opportunity to find compromises in areas that are not actually vital.

The biggest problem of the Yellowstone bison is perhaps ours as well—they live in the twenty-first century. There is no unclaimed land where bison can be free from human interference. My intent is to explore the uncharted middle ground for opportunities to benefit Yellowstone's bison, while respecting the vital interests of area ranchers. One direction is to support the development of a bison-specific brucellosis vaccine that, over time, could eliminate the unfounded concern by ranchers of brucellosis bacteria being transmitted to cattle. A "clean" herd will also allow excess Yellowstone bison (currently about one thousand) the opportunity to join other herds, a much better option than the current one, summary execution.

Veryl: The Buffalo Field Campaign is a valiant group of folks who constantly keep the plight of the Yellowstone bison before the public. They are on the front lines year round facing the often inhumane treatment of the bison as they attempt to do what every other herd animal in Yellowstone does—migrate to lower elevations to give birth. I have a deep respect for the BFC but join Roger in feeling that the eradication of brucellosis is vital to stop the unfair treatment of the Yellowstone herd and address the concerns of the ranchers.

Another opportunity is available only with the Yellowstone herd—the opportunity to study buffalo behavior. After the great slaughter of the 1800s, buffalo were "reinvented" as domesticated herd animals. Bison somehow slipped through the cracks of wildlife research. Only the Yellowstone herd can provide true insight to unmanaged behavior.

RDR: Writing *A Buffalo in the House* certainly changed me in several ways, including enlarging my appreciation of this extraordinary animal and the natural world in general, and enlarging my historical perspective through my research into an often forgotten, and very tragic, period in our country's past. Also, the integrity with which you've led your own lives with animals has been an inspiration. How has the experience with Charlie, and the experience of being written about, changed *you*?

Roger: Charlie opened up a new chapter of understanding for me and for many others who met him. By having a personal relationship with a bison, I better appreciated that every animal of every species is an individual. Charlie was who he was, an example of the completely honest nature of the animal world.

I first viewed our bottle-raising of Charlie as an opportunity to know and relate with an animal that I otherwise wouldn't have the opportunity to know. Our goal with Charlie was to reintroduce him to his own kind and have him become part of a herd. After his injury, when release was impossible, we formed a bond. To Charlie, I was his mother, his (hard-to-convince) mate, and, since he was a bull, his rival. I accepted the first role, avoided the second, and delicately dealt with the third.

Veryl: I have raised many animals over the years as a means of sculpting from life. Each one has brought a deeper understanding of that species. Raising Charlie and sculpting directly from him enabled me to bring a different point of view to a buffalo sculpture.

1. Before reading *A Buffalo in the House,* how much did you know about buffalo? What new things did you learn about the species' history in America?

2. On page 17, R. D. Rosen writes: "When the British explored Virginia in 1733, they found hordes of wild buffalo, 'so gentle and undisturbed' that men could almost pet them." How do you think our lives would be different today if the buffalo were able to continue their dominance of the American landscape?

3. Charlie came into Veryl and Roger's family because of Veryl's need, and because he'd been abandoned. Have you ever adopted an orphaned pet? What circumstances led you to decide to welcome an abandoned animal into your home?

4. Roger Brooks did not expect to fall in love with Charlie. In fact, he first thought of Charlie as "Veryl's baby bison." But he soon realized he had become quite attached without knowing it. In what ways can you relate to Roger's experience? Have you ever fallen in love—with a pet *or a person*—unexpectedly? In what ways do you think we love animals and people differently?

5. In nineteenth-century America, politicians were chiefly concerned with removing impediments to westward expansion—and the buffalo (live ones) and American Indians stood in their

way and suffered accordingly. Today, what other populations—
animal or human—are being threatened or destroyed in the
name of "progress"?

6. Can you imagine any other "solution" to the problems presented by tens of millions of buffalo covering the American
plains in the nineteenth century? Or was the Great Buffalo
Slaughter inevitable?

7. Buffalo are making something of a comeback these days.
Many people would like to see buffalo once again roam the
Great Plains, especially in economically depressed areas, where
they might attract tourist dollars and also revitalize the soil. Do
you think this is a good idea?

8. A growing number of vegetarians highlight the harsh treatment of animals farmed for consumption as their chief reason
for removing meat from their diets. Has reading this book
changed your perspective on eating meat? If so, what would
you attribute to that change?

9. Even owners of large breed dogs have empathized with
Roger and Veryl's plight as Charlie became a bit too big for the
house. If you own a pet, what challenges did you face integrat-
ing that pet into your new home? Was it easy to establish
boundaries—where it could roam, what it could do?

10. What role do you think Charlie played in his family—aside
from sculpture model? If you have a pet, how does it fit into

your family? If you have more than one pet, how did the other(s) respond to new additions?

11. Roger and Veryl are quick to mention that Charlie actually brought them closer together. Does your pet bring you closer to the other members of your family?

12. Because of his unique upbringing, perhaps the biggest challenge Charlie faced was an identity crisis—he didn't quite distinguish that Roger and Veryl were humans and that he was a buffalo. In what ways did your upbringing inform your sense of identity, of who you are and where you belong? What adjustments did you find were necessary as you got older?

13. Roger and Veryl went to great odds to get Charlie to their home, to raise him, and to care for him under some intense circumstances. How much would you risk to bring an animal into your home? And what would you be willing to do to save its life?

R. D. ROSEN's books include *Psychobabble* (a word he coined) and the Edgar Award–winning mystery novel *Strike Three You're Dead*. His career as a humorist spans *The Generic News* on PBS, *Saturday Night Live*, and HBO's *Not Necessarily the News*. He is the creator and co-author of the bestselling series of "Bad" books: *Bad Cat, Bad Dog, Bad Baby*, and *Bad President*.

He is currently at work on a book about apes in show business. His e-mail address is rydean49@aol.com.